Also by Myra Cohn Livingston

THE MALIBU AND OTHER POEMS
(*A Margaret K. McElderry Book*)   1972

When You Are Alone/
It Keeps You Capone

When You Are Alone/
It Keeps You Capone

An Approach to

Creative Writing with Children

Myra Cohn Livingston

Atheneum *New York* *1973*

The author wishes to acknowledge the following publishers for permission to reprint:

"The Dream" and "Tea Party" from *Windy Morning*, copyright 1953 by Harry Behn. Reprinted by permission of Harcourt Brace Jovanovich, Inc.

"If things were better" by Issa, from *Cricket Songs: Japanese Haiku*, translated and © 1964 by Harry Behn. Reprinted by permission of Harcourt Brace Jovanovich, Inc.

"The Bird of Night" from *The Bat-Poet* by Randall Jarrell, copyright © Macmillan Publishing Co., Inc. 1963, 1964.

"The Pasture" from *You Come Too* by Robert Frost. Copyright 1939, © 1967, 1969 by Holt, Rinehart and Winston, Inc. Reprinted by permission of Holt, Rinehart and Winston, Inc.

"Poem." Copyright 1932 and renewed © 1960 by Langston Hughes. Reprinted from *The Dream Keeper and Other Poems*, by Langston Hughes, by permission of Alfred A. Knopf, Inc.

"At the door of my own little hovel" by A. E. Housman is reprinted by permission of Charles Scribner's Sons from *My Brother, A. E. Housman*. Copyright 1937, 1938 Laurence Housman; renewal copyright © 1965, 1966 Lloyds Bank Limited; The Society of Authors as the literary representative of the Estate of A. E. Housman; and Jonathan Cape Ltd., publishers of Laurence Housman's *My Brother, A. E. Housman*.

"Teapots and Quails" from *Teapots and Quails and Other New Nonsenses* by Edward Lear. Reprinted by permission of John Murray (Publishers) Ltd.

"King Tut," Copyright © 1961 by X. J. Kennedy from the book *Nude Descending a Staircase*. Reprinted by permission of Doubleday & Company, Inc.

"The Stamp" from *Platero and I* by Juan Ramon Jimenez (translated by Eloise Roach), University of Texas Press, 1957.

Copyright © 1973 by Myra Cohn Livingston
All rights reserved
Library of Congress catalog card number 73-80758
ISBN 0-689-10579-7
Published simultaneously in Canada by McClelland and Stewart Ltd.
Manufactured in the United States of America by
H. Wolff, New York
Designed by Kathleen Carey
First Edition

"CREATIVE WRITING, POETRY—*where* do I start?"

This question arises as teachers approach a creative writing unit. It is a simple one to ask yet a most complex one to answer.

Too often, teachers seeking a structure within which to teach creative writing begin with poetic forms and techniques. This "mechanical" approach can inhibit rather than foster children's imaginations. It can actually interfere with the students' potential for creative effort, because it forces them to fit their creative responses to a particular form (for example, rhyme and rhythms) too soon. The results of such a premature effort are often mass-produced, cliché-ridden statements that serve as poor substitutes for the emergence of freshly observed, individually felt expressions.

As teachers at the University Elementary School at the University of California, Los Angeles, we also had been asking ourselves, "Where do we start in teaching creative writing?" and "What should children do that first day, and each following day, to release their creativity?" Like many teachers, we had found ourselves questioning an approach to poetry based only on forms and techniques. We felt there must be some other way to release rather than restrict the creative force within each child.

We found some answers to our questions when we were given an opportunity to work with Myra Livingston, a gifted poet and writer, who volunteered to work daily with our classroom of children at the University Elementary School. This experience, most rewarding for children and teachers alike, helped us to generate new answers to our questions: "Where do we start?" and "What will free each child's creativity?"

Mrs. Livingston vividly demonstrated with children at our school the success of starting with what each child brings to the classroom every day: (1) a wealth of *experiences* that barrage his senses every moment, for example, the sensation of going higher and higher on a playground swing; (2) the force of deep *feelings* about all he experiences, such as the pure joy of floating cleanly through space on a swing; and (3) the impact of his *imagination* and *inventiveness* by which the swing can become a spaceship taking him to unknown places. Experiences, feelings, imagination, and inventiveness—these are the substance of creative writing, the real content of poetry. This is where the poetic feast should start and it should constitute its main course.

Form and technique should be part of our creative writing fare but, as our experiences with Mrs. Livingston have shown us, they are secondary. The forms, the tools and techniques, serve as the utensils and dishes for serving the food at the feast. The food of creativity—its very essence—is the feeling felt and expressed as children learn to speak from their hearts, to say what they really want to and not what they think others—their teachers, parents, and peers—want them to say.

What then, if we re-evaluate our teaching of creative writing? "What, then," asks Myra Livingston in her article "Literature, Creativity and Imagination" (*Childhood Education*, April 1972), "if we commit ourselves to the imagination of each child who enters our classroom or library? This potential for arousing the imagination," she continues, "to sense new relationships, to seize hold of them, to work creatively is assuredly there. And somehow we must find new ways, new methods by which we may bring literature to our young people."

In this book, you, too, can share with Myra Livingston—as we did at the University Elementary School—her insights and her experiences with children and teachers when she tried these "new ways" and "new methods" to excite each child's creative potential. Here, a teacher will find suggested objectives and learning opportunities, with a stimulating selection of examples from children's own writing. Here are some answers to that very important question: "Where do I start when I teach creative writing?"

—Ann de la Sota and Cynthiana Brown
  Teachers at the University Elementary School
  University of California, Los Angeles

Acknowledgments

IT IS NOT POSSIBLE for me to thank everyone who has raised my spirits and given me a chance to work. But I should like to mention a few.

My particular thanks to Siddie Joe Johnson, formerly Coordinator of Children's Services at the Dallas Public Library, who gave me my first chance to teach; to Natalie Murray and Murietta Swain of the Lamplighter School in Dallas, Texas; to Mattie Ruth Moore of the Dallas Independent School District and Laurie Dudley at the Dallas Public Library; to the Dallas Museum of Contemporary Arts and the Junior League of Dallas; and to Sawnie Aldredge of the Aldredge Book Store and Decherd Turner of the Bridwell Library at Southern Methodist University.

Of those who have helped me most recently, I offer special thanks to Kenneth Peters, Superintendent of the Beverly Hills Unified School District, and Dr. Isabel Dible, Director of Elementary Education, for their belief in my work; to Dr. Madeline Hunter, principal of University Elementary School at the University of California, Los Angeles, and Ann de la Sota, Cynthiana Brown, and Carolyn Horovitz at the University Elementary School; to Dr. Malcolm Douglass, Priscilla Fenn, and Winifred Ragsdale of the Claremont Graduate School; to Charlotte Davis of the Santa Barbara County Schools, Betty Ryder of the Pasadena Public Library, Helen Fuller of the Long Beach Public Library, and Jerome Cushman at U.C.L.A.; to the Los Angeles County Museum of Art; to Gladys Zweibach and Toby Omens of the Beverly Hills Public Library.

My thanks also to Mae Durham, at the University of California, Berkeley, for encouraging me in my speaking and writing; to Nancy Larrick, Isabel Wilner, Donna Harsh, Virginia Reid, Elliot Landau, Herbert Sandberg, Sister Margaret Clare, Lee Bennett Hopkins, and the many people of NCTE, ACE, IRA, CLA, and ALA who have given me a chance to express my views; to the Children's Book Council, the Southern California Council on Literature for Children and Young People, and the Texas Institute of Letters; to those publications, including *The Horn Book*, *Top of the News*, *Childhood Education*, and *The Wilson Library Journal*, that have included my articles; and to the hundreds of people who have invited me to PTA meetings and book fairs, as well as classrooms and libraries, throughout the country.

Although I have never met them, I feel that I must also mention Hughes Mearns, John Ciardi, Archibald MacLeish, X. J. Kennedy, and George Steiner—for they have, through their books, gathered ideas together in my head that I, in turn, have given back to the children whom I have taught.

I am thankful to Robert Fitzgerald and Horace Gregory for the words they gave me many years ago at Sarah Lawrence College that have not been forgotten.

More than anyone else, perhaps, I thank Margaret K. McElderry for all she has meant to me.

And to the countless children everywhere, thanks, for being themselves.

Contents

When You Are Alone/
It Keeps You Capone

1: By Way of an Observation

IT HAPPENED at the Claremont Colleges Reading Conference during some sessions with several hundred elementary school children who came, by choice, to spend an hour doing creative writing.

As is my custom, I had sent the children outside with paper and pencil to observe their surroundings. A number of children had spotted one of those curious, old-fashioned lamps that stood in the yard.

> I have a lamp
> I use it when it's dark and damp
> It has a very good light
> It shines very bright
> My lamp

wrote Margaret.
Jennie's poem was entitled "Lanterns":

> Blink! Blink! Flicker! Blink!
> You wonder if it ever goes out;
> A lighted jail house, a blurred sun;
> A lone star.

Ken turned in this one:

> The lamppost gives me security,
> Guiding me through the night,
> Giving me the needed light
> To get me home quite alright.
>
> The lamppost is there for the day too,
> I swing around it for something to do.
> The lamp post is like Linus's blanket,
> Something need by me, I thank it.

Margaret's practical approach, Jennie's images of a jail house, a sun, and a star, and Ken's rather amazing simile all testify to the varying richness of children's minds and to their varying abilities to respond to the world around them. We can observe in Margaret's verse (for it is hardly poetry) that poverty of imagery that so often comes out as factual statement, and which arouses in the teacher the wish to get into the child's thoughts and imagination. How can we reach her, we ask, to help her make of her statement a poem? How can we find out whether she uses a lamp only when it's "damp"? Dare we suggest to her that she may also use the lamp when it is *dry*, and that she probably harbors the mistaken notion that rhyme is an absolute necessity for a poem? How will we lead her to recognize that when she rhymes "light" with "bright" the rhyme is fluent and sensible, but that she probably has chosen "damp" either because it was the first rhyme she thought of or because it is more intelligible than, say, "vamp" or "ramp" or "camp"? There is always the possibility that she will defend herself, however, telling us that she never uses a lamp unless it is damp. In this case we must respect her wishes. We will, however, tuck this information into our heads so that when we read her next poem we will be alert to her use of rhyme at the expense of sense.

Would we be able to teach Margaret, after a period of time, that rhyme is not poetry but merely an element, a tool, of poetry, brilliant and exciting when well used, but dull, confining, and even ludicrous when poorly employed?

We do not need to worry about overuse of rhyme in Jennie's case. She has said, we may be sure, what she wanted to say, and furthermore she would seem to have a natural feel for rhythm. In time, after seeing more of her writing, we might be able to venture a few suggestions. The second line might be stronger without the word "You," and there is the slightest hint of cliché in the image of the "lone star" (if one has a Texas background). But it is a good first effort and deserves praise.

We're back to rhyme in Ken's poem. He likes it. He feels a need of it. So be it. He has overdone it a bit in the first stanza ("night"/"light"/"alright"), but we would eventually teach him something about the couplet and the quatrain so that his poems would be more balanced. We will work with him to point out that there is no need for the word "security," for he has *shown* security in the first stanza and reiterated this in the lamppost-blanket simile. There is a beautiful second line in the second stanza! How boylike! How natural! I cannot remember ever seeing "blanket" and "thank it" rhymed before, but this, too, is fresh and in keeping with the spirit of the stanza.

And praise be for the error of "need" instead of the more correct "needed." When one is in the throes of creativity, let punctuation and grammar go by the boards—these can always be corrected later.

Most germane, however, to an approach to teaching creative writing is another poem written that day by another girl named Margaret.

Lamps are on
Some stay on all night
for people to see
because they give off light.

When you are alone
it keeps you capone.

The first stanza is a first-rate example of that sort of creative writing that we all must recognize as poor. A lack of meaning in the imagery, an insistence upon factual statement, and a complete absence of tone, of the writer's viewpoint or feelings, are scarcely offset by the binding use of rhyme. There is a faint glimmer in the second stanza, however, that the child will make herself heard: "When you are alone," she starts out, and we wait, hopefully, to hear something new, something fresh, something of her feelings. Unfortunately, we are disappointed not only that she shuts the door on the listener, but that she does it with meaningless rhyme. We, the listeners, have been cheated from beginning to end, but more important, the child herself has not been able to express her feelings, her thoughts. What is it like when you are alone? What "keeps you"? What happens when you need to see at night? What do you need to say? Is the lamp comforting? Are you fearful? Do you like the dark? So many, many questions unanswered, so many possibilities and potentialities unexplored.

The chances are that one hour in Claremont is all I will ever know of Ken, Jennie, and the two Margarets. But it is because of them, their teachers, and those countless thousands whom I have met around this country that I wish to share my experiences in the teaching of creative writing.

One does not *teach* creative writing, of course, but merely works at developing sensibilities and nurturing them.

One encourages expression, true and meaningful expression (as distinguished from factual statement); reads poetry, introduces forms, and speaks about the elements and tools of poetry and how meaning is to be found in poetry, so that each child will, we hope, find a form that best expresses his own thoughts and feelings.

During the past fifteen years, I have attended hundreds of book fairs, read numerous volumes of children's writing, talked to thousands of teachers, and spoken about poetry and creative writing to elementary and high school groups as well as university and college groups. I have been employed by school districts, conducted classes and clubs at libraries, and been in touch with children of kindergarten through high school age, and I have learned as much from these young people as I have been able to teach them.

I am mindful of the teacher's monumental job—teaching children to read, to spell, to fathom mathematics, to learn history and science and languages. I stand in awe of the teacher. At the same time I know the value to the individual of being given a chance to express himself in creative writing. It is to those dedicated teachers who wish to offer creative writing, but who know little of poetry or how to approach it, that I offer an account of my own experiences.

In Randall Jarrell's *The Bat-Poet*, the little bat, who sees things quite differently than the other bats, admires the songs of the mockingbird. The mockingbird, ever "full of himself," has consented to listen to the bat's poem about an owl who almost killed him. The bat eagerly awaits the mockingbird's response to the poem.

> "Why, I like it," said the mockingbird. "Technically, it's quite accomplished. The way you change the rhyme-scheme's particularly effective."

The bat said: "It is?"

"Oh yes," said the mockingbird. "And it was clever of you to have that last line two feet short."

The bat said blankly: "Two feet short?"

"It's two feet short," said the mockingbird a little impatiently. "The next-to-the-last line's iambic pentameter, and the last line's iambic trimeter."

The bat looked so bewildered that the mockingbird said in a kind voice: "An iambic foot has one weak syllable and one strong syllable; the weak one comes first. That last line of yours has six syllables and the one before it has ten: when you shorten the last line like that it gets the effect of the night holding its breath."

"I didn't know that," the bat said. "I just made it like holding your breath."

"To be sure, to be sure!" said the mockingbird. "I enjoyed your poem very much. When you've made up some more do come round and say me another."

The bat said that he would, and fluttered home to his rafter. Partly he felt very good—the mockingbird had liked his poem—and partly he felt just terrible. He thought: "Why, I might as well have said it to the bats. What do I care how many feet it has? The owl nearly kills me, and he says he likes the rhyme-scheme!" He hung there upside down, thinking bitterly. After a while he said to himself: "The trouble isn't making poems, the trouble's finding somebody that will listen to them."

Later, the bat has occasion to say the poem to a chipmunk, hoping to interest him in having his own portrait done in verse, "for only six crickets."

A shadow is floating through the moonlight.
Its wings don't make a sound.

> Its claws are long, its beak is bright.
> Its eyes try all the corners of the night.
>
> It calls and calls: all the air swells and heaves
> And washes up and down like water.
> The ear that listens to the owl believes
> In death. The bat beneath the eaves,
>
> The mouse beside the stone are still as death—
> The owl's air washes them like water.
> The owl goes back and forth inside the night,
> And the night holds its breath.

He said his poem and the chipmunk listened attentively; when the poem was over the chipmunk gave a big shiver and said, "It's terrible, just terrible! Is there really something like that at night?"

Later, the bat starts on his verse portrait of the chipmunk.

But somehow he kept coming back to the poem about the owl, and what the chipmunk had said, and how he'd looked. "*He* didn't say any of that two-feet short stuff," the bat thought triumphantly; "*he* was scared."

How many mockingbirds fail to be scared—to sense the force that elicits emotion and imagination? How many teachers, so concerned with the rhyme scheme and the rhythm, accept these elements as substitutes for the meaning? How many children, like the little bat, must keep their poems and flights of imagination to themselves, because there is a mockingbird so puffed up with his own song, his own dictates, that the real stuff of creation never gets through?

"The universal need of the young," says Dr. Harold Taylor, "is for a mode of expression through which they

7

can say to the world something of their own in a way which is their own. . . ."

Poetry and creative writing are but one form of expression; it is of this, and to Margaret—alone, and in need of soaring above *capone*—that I wish to speak.

2: *To Share and Share and Share Some More*

IN A CLASSROOM of thirty second-graders at the Seventy-fourth Street School in Los Angeles, where I had been invited to share poetry, we made up a poem. Rita, madly waving her hand, thought that a good nonsense word with which to start might be "HOCCHI." Howard suggested that the next word could be "BOCCHI," and perhaps it was Mammon who created the next word, "POCCHINOCCHI."

HOCCHI BOCCHI POCCHINOCCHI
HOCCHI BOCCHI POCCHINOCCHI
HOCCHI BOCCHI POCCHINOCCHI

Deirdre helped with the last line:

ALL FALL DOWN AND LIBERACE——

We clapped our poem and we danced our poem, and when the children *had* all fallen down, they rose to choose from an assortment of colored paper, brand new crayons with sharp points, and pencils and pens—materials with which to write their own individual poems.

9

I dreamed I saw a ghost,
I were frightened.
My mother came in.

wrote Alice. Could an earlier reading of Harry Behn's poem "The Dream" have had anything to do with this?

One night I dreamed
I was lost in a cave,
A cave that was empty
And dark and cool,
And down into nothing
I dropped a stone
And it fell like a star
Far and alone,
And a sigh arose
The sigh of a wave
Rippling the heart
Of a sunless pool.

And after a while
In my dream I dreamed
I climbed a sky
That was high and steep
And still as a mountain
Without a cave,
As still as water
Without a wave,
And on that hill
Of the sun it seemed
That all sad sounds
In the world fell asleep.

There is no question that our collective class poem "HOCCHI BOCCHI" sprang from the delight with nonsense words inspired by Behn's "Tea Party."

> Mister Beedle Baddlebug,
> Don't bandle up in your boodlebag
> Or numble in your jimblejug,
> Now eat your nummy tiffletag
> Or I will never invite you
> To tea again with me. Shoo!

The sharing of poetry, wherever one is, in the classroom or library or at home, is intrinsic to the development of the imagination and the humanization of child and adult alike. This is also true of much prose, with which one can stir the minds of young people, as well, provided it bears a relationship to the goal at hand—to stimulate, to arouse, to embolden. In selecting poetry as a basis for creative writing development, one chooses those poems that embody particular elements of form, or voice, as they relate to special needs. One considers, as well, the age and sophistication of the child.

Unfortunately, most children today are unschooled in poetry. They have heard verse and macaronics and ditties and jingles in the many television commercials that bombard them daily. Yet this exposure is not without a certain advantage, for if nothing else rhythmic patterns that they may hear nowhere else pervade these singing advertisements. Many children have never heard Mother Goose in the home and acquire some inner feeling for metrics only from the lead or tag tunes of the situation comedy or the most persuasive commercials:

> A horse is a horse, of course, of course. . . .

> Pepsi-Cola hits the spot,
> Twelve-ounce bottle, that's a lot, . . .

This is not to suggest that we offer these jingles to young people as models, but rather to urge that we accept them

11

as part of life and in the absence of any other starting point seize hold of their metrical (and sometimes rhyming) possibilities. What they lack, of course, is a tone, a voice, a quality that can never be captured by didacticism or commercialism.

I am far more concerned about children who read so-called books from five-and-ten-cent stores and inferior commercial book clubs, wherein the worst sort of prose abounds, than I am with the child who knows only a few jingles, and therefore comes to poetry and writing almost a *tabula rasa*. For there is natural rhythm with which all children are endowed that can be brought to the fore, fostered, and encouraged in the yet undeveloped mind and body. I must here stress the body and its own rhythms, for it bears very heavily on the entire range of poetry to which children respond. Our hearts pulsate each to its own beat, our legs walk or run or jump or hop in a particular cadence, and it is natural that some of us should come alive to T. S. Eliot's Jellicle cats:

> *Jellicle Cats come out tonight,*
> *Jellicle Cats come one come all:*
> *The Jellicle Moon is shining bright—*
> *Jellicles come to the Jellicle Ball.*

whereas others of us might respond more directly to the less buoyant, more mysterious Macavity:

> Macavity's a Mystery Cat: he's called the Hidden
> Paw—
> For he's the master criminal who can defy the Law.

We are all geared to different beats, different tunes, and this fact alone should guide us not only in sharing poetry with young people but in understanding why there is such a divergency of ability when it comes to writing poetry. That light-hearted metrical foot the anapest ($\smile\smile/$), the basis for the limerick form, cannot, alas, be grasped easily by a worried or distressed child; indeed, there are days and hours when the teacher feels at odds with the gaiety of such a form.

I often find myself in this kind of predicament. Armed with a stack of anthologies, on my way to share poetry with children in a classroom or a library, I am never sure until I see the group, and find myself settled in the room, just what I will share. There is a pulse that must be taken, a mood established. The day may be filled with sun, or smog may be smarting our eyes. The children may be at the beginning of a school day, or weary at the end of a long session with history; they may be refreshed after lunch, or panting from a game of baseball. So, too, with the teacher, whose own state of mind may suggest a need for levity, or for a quiet, more sober mood.

Perhaps this is the reason why recordings and audio-visual aids, although useful at times, can never take the place of one's own freedom of choice and expression. We are blessed today with such a wealth of fine anthologies and volumes of individual poets that one has to spend only a little time to find a poem that will satisfy the particular needs of the time and the place, and, one hopes, of the children listening.

But poetry—the sharing of it—is not a TV show, a movie, a circus, or a popularity contest. Many of us make the mistake, as I did at first, of being downcast or frustrated when a specially chosen poem lays the proverbial egg. May I stress that it is virtually impossible to know what poem may strike a responsive chord in a given child. One is not out to capture every child, but the *individual* child who may have need for a thought or a feeling for which he has heretofore found no words. Educators who feel that it is possible to choose one poem or a group of poems by which all other poetry can be perceived and understood will never succeed. There is no body of work that will encompass all rhythms of the mind and body of all persons at all times. We must, instead, make a wide and diverse selection, and trust that, even if not at a given moment, some one poem we have read or recited will later hit its mark. But wild applause is not part of the picture. Let us leave that to entertainers!

I have found it important, however, to introduce poems of levity immediately, for two very different reasons. In the first place, we, as teachers (and not incidentally human beings), need the assurance that we can relate to the group. We do not want to fall flat. We need some spark from the children's faces, some laughter or at least an amused smile, especially when facing a group of older children whose former experience with poetry may well have turned them off or tuned them out. In many schools poetry is introduced to fulfill a requirement that has nothing whatever to do with pure enjoyment.

But of prime importance (and far beyond the boost to our ego) is the knowledge that in presenting humorous poetry we are counteracting that misconception held by most adults, and therefore by the children who listen to them, that poetry has to do only with Beauty, Truth, Wisdom, Purity, and the like; that it is something reserved for Sunday School; words that exhort us only to live up to our highest nature. For although we do strive toward our best and hope to impart something of this to young people, they need to know (and so do we) that we all have our frailties. We cannot always be serious and stalwart. We like to laugh, and we need a good joke.

King Tut
Crossed over the Nile
On steppingstones of crocodile.

King Tut!
His mother said,
Come here this minute!
You'll get wet feet.
King Tut is dead

And now King Tut
Tight as a nut
Keeps his big fat Mummy shut.

King Tut,   tut, tut.

X. J. Kennedy's poem lets us know that poetry can also be made up of human error, of misbehaving, of everyday exclamations, of the comeuppance that sons impose on their mothers. Nothing is alien to poetry and poetry is not sacrosanct. It is more than daffodils and lying pensive on a couch and moral virtues, as reading only Wordsworth might lead us to believe. We can point out to the older child, for example, that when the Reverend Charles Lutwidge Dodgson, as Lewis Carroll, wrote "The Aged Aged Man" (in *Through the Looking Glass, and What Alice Found There*), he was poking fun at the high moral tone of Wordsworth in "Resolution and Independence," suggesting that "thinking of a plan/To dye one's whiskers green" is probably as worthy an endeavor as musing upon "dim sadness," "blind thoughts," and a leech-gatherer. And when Carroll tells us,

Speak roughly to your little boy
And beat him when he sneezes,
He only does it to annoy
Because he knows it teases . . . ,

he is counteracting the virtuous pomposity of such didactic exhortations as

> Speak gently to the little child.
> Its love be sure to gain.
> Teach it in accents soft and mild.
> It may not long remain.

It is of vital importance to let young people know that nothing in the human condition is alien to poetry. In the words of the great Chilean poet Pablo Neruda:

> It is well, at certain hours of the day and night, to look closely at the world of objects at rest. Wheels that have crossed long, dusty distances with their mineral and vegetable burdens, sacks from the coalbins, barrels and baskets, handles and hafts for the carpenter's tool chest. From them flow the contacts of man with the earth, like a text for all harassed lyricists. The used surface of things, the air, tragic at times, pathetic at others, of such things—all lend a curious attractiveness to the reality of the world that should not be underprized. . . .
>
> Let that be the poetry we search for: worn with the hand's obligations, as by acids, steeped in sweat and in smoke, smelling of lilies and urine, spattered diversely by the trades that we live by, inside the law or beyond it.

The search for poems to share is unending. So is our commitment to share them. But it is an important beginning.

3: *Creative Writing: Its Tools*

A PIECE OF notebook paper, punched with holes for a binder and neatly lined in blue with a pink margin line, is one thing. A blank piece of paper is quite another. The first, in the context of school work, bespeaks careful attention to penmanship, spelling, paragraphing, punctuation—the myriad of disciplines with which composition writing abounds.

But the blank piece of paper suggests freedom, imagination—one can make of it, properly folded, a paper airplane or boat, or cut out paper dolls or make a picture. One can also use it for writing, especially the sort of writing we call creative. Here there is no need for correct spelling, neat margins, or exact punctuation. There is simply the glorious freedom to write as one wants, in slant lines or in a circle, in large letters or small. One can use a crayon or pencil or pen in black or red—or purple.

When it is time for creative writing, it is time to put out colored paper, construction paper, yellow or blue or green second sheets, even old paper sacks, and perhaps even small note pads for the child who likes to write in a diminutive, secret fashion. Whatever is available and suggests the freedom to create is wanted here.

Some of us like ink, blue or black; some prefer a fine line pencil, and others function best with a soft, heavy lead. Some children gravitate to brightly colored crayons. The point is, of course, that each of us is an individual. The cheapest grade of yellow second sheets and a black typewriter ribbon or a heavy felt marker arouse, in this writer, flights of great fancy. Perhaps a clean white sheet of paper and a fine line pen may suit another.

I always ask when I go into a classroom that a variety of papers and writing instruments be made available. I have discovered that some children will prefer blue to yellow, or white to pink. What is important is that the choice be offered—even orange paper at Halloween, or green and red at Christmastime—for what will arouse the imagination of one will stifle another. It may be that some children will prefer lined paper; I have seen children take rulers from their desks in order to draw the lines with which they feel more comfortable. Let us stay clear of the pristine sheet of notebook paper that literally screams Neatness, Correct Spelling, Punctuation. There will be time, later, to go back and correct all of our errors, to put into proper form the poem we wish to share with others.

I am indebted to the poet Horace Gregory for introducing me—as a junior at Sarah Lawrence College—to the value of the observation sheet. It was a rather complicated procedure involving many field trips and page after page of writing, as well as countless miles and hours. I remember one event vividly: a trip to New York to see *The Duchess of Malfi* at the Ethel Barrymore Theatre. On the right-hand side of the observation sheet was a list of all the facts about the trip: what time the train left; a description of the train and where I sat; the appearance of the people on the train, of the conductor; the smells of the station and later, the subway or bus; the appearance of the theater, the exact time the curtain went up, what action took place upon the stage, what the audience looked like, and how they reacted to the play. This record, taking up page after page, was labeled *Objective*.

On the left-hand side, however, was a column entitled *Subjective*, and it recorded what is intrinsic to creative writing, my own feelings about what was happening, thus:

Subjective	*Objective*
	I walked up three stairs, directly against the wall and had to climb over four people, three women and one man to get to the seat. There was a dark velvet drape hung over the pole in front of the seats which brushed against my legs. It was difficult to get across because all of these people made no attempt to move. I found an empty seat next to me, put down the book, Gorky's *Reminiscences*, an apple, a bunch of yellow mums
why I hate to go to the theater after doing other things	wrapped in brown paper and the black calf shoulder bag I was carrying on the seat, took off my coat, folded it over the rail, sat down and picked up my belongings. Took off sunglasses and put

Subjective

Objective

on regular frames. I looked around the theater for a minute.

I say large in comparison to some other New York theaters I have seen . . . although one would hardly compare it to Carnegie Hall, or the Shrine in Los Angeles.

It is a large theater

magnificent chandelier . . . usually don't care for them . . . the roseate light creates the kind of feeling in Aunt Blanche's living room . . . I see that statue of the woman reclining on the bench (wasn't it bronze?) and Frances had her wedding picture taken there. "Life is Just a Bowl of Cherries" on the piano . . . the blue and white slip covers in summer. . . .

There is an orchestra floor, and a balcony. A large chandelier, lighted, hangs from the ceiling. A roseate light floods everywhere.

```
toboganning in the
snow . . . Joy was
ugly . . . whipped
jello . . .
```

It is not too difficult to see that the subjective feelings noted here constitute the matter most valuable to creative writing: feelings that transform a roseate light into a return to early childhood and a flood of memories.

Such an observation sheet, though valuable for a college or even a high school student, is too complicated for grammar school children; over the years, therefore, I have adapted it for immediate use in the classroom. I will, as early as third grade, ask the children to fold a piece of paper in half, and look about the room for some object to describe. There is probably no schoolroom without an American flag, so let us use this object as an example. We will also change the headings to read *What I Saw* and *What I Thought About What I Saw*

What I Thought About What I Saw	*What I Saw*
	American Flag
Child 1: I think about our men in Viet Nam	red and white stripes field of blue
Child 2: I think about a parade	50 stars
Child 3: We pledge allegiance every morning	on a black pole made of cloth
Child 4: from the first day of Kindergarten til your out of high school you say the flag salute or at least your suppose to	

What I Thought About What I Saw	*What I Saw*
	Pencil
Child 5: I write with it.	red
Child 6: Looks like a candy cane	four inches long black lead at one end
Child 7: reminds me of a stick of peppermint	eraser, pink used for writing
Child 8: could be a rocket going to the moon	

The subjective observations given here are typical of those I have collected over the years, but it should not be difficult to note that of the eight examples cited, a few burst with potential for creative writing. The child who made the observation about saying the flag salute elaborated upon this later. A rebel, she has remained a source of consternation to all. The child who could think of the pencil only as a writing tool has also been a continual challenge, for he can think only in terms of facts. The candy cane and peppermint observations are the beginnings of simile and metaphor. The boy for whom the pencil becomes a rocket is, as one might suspect, a child who shows promise.

Observation sheets should not be confined to the classroom alone. If the weather is good, one can send the children out to observe several different objects. At a school like the University Elementary School, the experimental school at the University of California, Los Angeles, where there are patios, paths among trees, and even a gully, the possibilities are countless. Inclement weather confines us to the classroom, but even in a light drizzle, a ten-minute walk on the school playground can be a source of inspiration. Angela, a fifth-grader at Fairburn Avenue School in West Los Angeles, wrote this:

What I Thought	*What I Saw*
like little ladies in black at department stores, always picking out the best of things. Reminds me of a girl I know. Easily scared by the bad things and flattered by the good.	the pidgons small cocky free
hard and cold. Spraying frozen liquid all over you like a thousand knives against my skin.	the water wet cold

Bambi, who also saw the "piegions," described them as "black and white, fat, short." Her subjective column noted, "makes me feel free, easy, glad that I'm on the ground on hot days and feel like flying on cool days." Dova noted a "pigon." "It's brown and black walks funny. Looks funny. I feel like flying when I see a pigon. I also love the way they walk with their heads bobing up and down."

The next step, of course, with observation charts, is to turn the observations and feelings into a poem, and the trick is to encourage the children to *use* the subjective feelings, for this is where creativity and individuality enter. It is amazing to note, however, that oftentimes a child who can make metaphorical observations of a poetic nature will completely forget them when writing a poem. Angela, who thought of pigeons as "little ladies in a department store," wrote:

> Little pidgons,
> almost human,
> always active,
> always movin'
> Seldom ever
> in this weather
> Stops to even

shake a feather ...
Stopping now
to pick up food
if their in that
kind of mood
Then suddenly
The quail comes
and spoils all
the pidgons fun,
Then in less
than half a second,
All the pidgons
are gone.

It is fascinating to see here how perfectly the rhythm of the birds is incorporated into the poem, yet how this child, except for the second line, decided to ignore as part of the poem the metaphorical observation she had made. It is also interesting to note how she feels a need of rhyme, and makes it for herself by the use of such words as "human" and "movin'" and "comes" and "fun" (imperfect ryhme), but also how she instinctively senses that rhyme should not be used at the end.

Jeffrey, who turned in no observation sheet that day, except for the caustic notation "Bird. It is black and white and it is a seagle," turned over his paper and wrote this:

The flowing
swift sudden
movement
of the Bird
Falling—down
into a hole the bird gose
down—whoever

nose where
he is off to in the
midnight light of
the moon

It is possible that Jeffrey needs no observation sheet, no bridge between fact and feeling. Some children seem able to plunge immediately into the realm of imagination that is the source of such a poem. But these are the exceptions. A larger percentage will need careful guidance and must be gently led to the point where they can see the difference. Fifth-graders and above are better able to distinguish between the two levels, whereas younger children often need more help. I have discovered that often it is better to substitute the words "it reminds me of" for "what I thought" or "what I felt." The only danger here is that the former can readily turn into a metaphor and simile contest between children at the expense of their true feelings. Mary O'Neill's *Hailstones and Halibut Bones* is a delightful book, yet, as overworked by teachers in countless classrooms, it becomes nothing more than a color association marathon ("red is a fire engine," "blue is the sky") rather than a true measure of a child's thoughts and emotions. In the same way, I have seen many teachers use a book of mine, *See What I Found*, in such a way that the objects named are merely named; no depth of feeling or association about the objects is touched in the children's writing. Such books may be useful springboards, but one must go beyond them.

The observation sheet, of course, is far more than things merely seen. Oftentimes I have used it with sounds and asked the children, outside the classroom, to listen to the sounds they hear at home or outdoors. A screaming fire engine may be "high" and "piercing" and make a child think of flames, of people hurt, of property destroyed; it may be the beginning of a poem or story easily done, but only if the child relates to that sound. Another child may be moved more by the sound of a gentle rain, or a sibling arguing or whining. The important point is that each child be allowed to choose his own sounds; therefore, this sort of exercise is best done as extra homework, once the pattern has been established.

On hearing water running in the bathtub
. . . washing my sister . . . Mary Cassatt's picture "The Bath" . . . a waterfall . . . the adventure of a boat going through a dangerous iceberg of bubble bath suds . . .

On hearing my mother playing the guitar when I'm in bed
. . . lullaby . . . my mother . . . a woman sitting in front of the fireplace. The woman has a red scarf on her head, a shawl and a long skirt. It is snowing outside, but inside it is warm. The woman is rocking a cradle with her foot and singing a song. . . .

Margot

Smelling and touching and tasting are all subjects for more observation sheets. One can begin in the classroom, of course; a bag of potato chips or a piece of candy given to each child will produce some astounding reactions. I have brought to some classes frankincense and myrrh for smelling. I have had children down on their hands and knees touching the floor, the cement in the playground, a rug, or a small patch of grass.

As I felt a pine cone
I felt as if one hundred needles were sticking all over

me. My whole body was a mass of prickles. I squirmed and itched it was so real. I dropped the pine cone and it stopped. Boy, what a funny feeling from a mere pine cone.

Lori

On touching marble
Reminds me of a great Roman and Grecian building and the gigantic 2 ton building blocks that were lifted by man . . .

Lloyd

On tasting a sweet potato
. . . the sweet potato was sweet. It was also hot, buttery, smooth and steamy. When you jabbed your fork into its warm, inviting meat and put it in your eager mouth and mushed it around for awhile, it gave you a feeling of warmth. . . .

Margot

After a few weeks of our work in creative writing at University Elementary School, Mrs. Ann de la Sota established an Observation Center in her classroom. A large poster proclaimed that this was an "OBSERVATION CENTER FOR POETRY. LOOK. HEAR. TOUCH. TASTE. SMELL." A table in the center contained boxes. In one were "Ocean Oddities," an assortment of shells, seaweed, and sand. A box called "Jazzy Junk" contained wool, clay, a screw, string, chalk, sandpaper. Another box contained vials of such things as orange peels and rose petals. For listening to there were a large conch shell and a pile of records near a phonograph. For looking at, there were a file box of pictures and a stack of books. But far more important was a notice urging the children to go outside and take a walk to use their senses. Mimeographed cards were provided for the children to record their experiences and observations. Thus, the sensitivity program became a part of a classroom where things meaningful to these particular children were available. This Observation Center was intelligently planned to make creative writing something that related to all subjects studied in the classroom. This freedom is not given in all schools, but it is certainly workable provided the teacher uses his or her own imagination, not relying on prepackaged units, but choosing the materials that relate best to her own students.

Perhaps one of the most valuable tools of all, and one that can be incorporated into the tightest environment, is the journal. A small notebook given to each child provides the greatest outlet of all for feelings and observations. It is important to explain, however, that a journal is more than a diary; it *can* record one's daily doings, but its more valuable asset is that it is a private record of how one feels about things. Many children, given a journal in which to write, will share entries with classmates or a teacher, but many will not. It does not matter. The point is that journals encourage the children to write, without need for grades or commendation or criticism.

During the years I have taught, I have been amazed at the different responses found in the journals children have shared, and at the willingness with which some children will share their entries, while to others the journal becomes a secret hiding place for hopes, fears, wishes, dreams. It is important, above all, that the teacher respect this need for privacy, for the journal is not intended to be an end in itself, but rather a spur to the outpouring of feelings. In many classes, depending on the age and maturity of the children, scarcely a journal entry is shared (on days when the teacher has requested that one be brought to class). In other groups, there is a joyous willingness to read whatever has been written.

From my own experience I would judge that this is oftentimes a matter of teacher-pupil relationship. The child who finds a teacher to be genuinely interested in and understanding of his feelings is willing to share. This is not unlike other relationships in life; we express our emotions to some individuals and hide them from others.

Peer acceptance can also play a part in this process; if one child shares his feelings in a classroom, others follow. The earlier in life this sort of expression can be introduced and fostered, the better, especially in light of the fact-orientation of many schools today. From third through sixth grade particularly, children must be constantly encouraged to express their feelings.

The following entries, from an Extended Day Class of the Beverly Hills Unified School District, attest to the frankness and feeling of most of the students:

> Our new math teacher is a living, walking, breathing, talking computer. . . . Our math teacher has blown a fuse. He has given us 400 pages of math to do with various instructions. "When you reach this problem yell, 'Big Numba is coming!' or 'I am a mathbird.' ". . . Big Numba is his "god." He is married to Great Circle and we are all his little digits. His favorite person is Luap Oksilahcim (his name spelled backwards), a hippie with long hair and dark glasses. . . .
>
> *Debra*

> I'm starting a rock 'n roll group and sometimes we have to take loads of music paper from our teacher's

closet. Don't worry . . . we'll pay it back when we make our first million.

December 31st, 12:00—It came like nothing. It was nothing. Iron pans strewn across the mahogany table—burning bells. Shrill sounds in my ear. Times Square on the television, thousands of people waving, screaming and yelling. But it was nothing—just a passing of time. The world is one year older now—one year closer to its death; violent death? "Auld Lang Syne" on the record player—coming out of the television—out of the piano. Dark sky and a cloudless night that won't even acknowledge the passing of something that never was, isn't and won't be! Time is stationary; it won't move, not even for a New Year's party. Only the people move and change each year—one year closer to death, and a celebration!

Lloyd

Monday, Nov. 14. Silence is an imaginary thing. It doesn't exist today and it may have never did. . . . Maybe someday the world will be quiet. Maybe we just won't do anything and we'll stop thinking. We will have reached quietness in its perfect state. . . .

Tues., Jan. 24. Before, I wrote that quietness wasn't or isn't what the world wants. Now I believe it is the solution to hate and misunderstanding. . . . What would happen if everyone stopped what they were doing, think of how we could improve ourselves, the whole world would improve about 100%. Not just a halt to the wars, or crimes, arguments, mistrusts, and conceit, but to throw down its weapons, meet the enemy and either go back fighting or have peace, work instead of steal, when a bank robber takes that time out, and give someone a chance before you mistrust them, and be friendly instead of snobbish, for it's harder to be conceited than to lay off on the insults. If two minutes of tranquillity could solve our problems then why hasn't this happened? Do we have to be perfect in order to want to be perfect? Or today, are we so different from one another that we can't understand each other.

Hate is the kindling for a fire called war. . . .

Mark

Blank paper, a pen or pencil or crayon, observation sheets, and a journal: with these we begin. What follows depends upon the richness of the child's imagination and the development of his sensibilities, in which we, as teachers, play an amazingly important part.

4: The First Poem Written: Its Voice

ONE OF THE pleasantest things about being a roving teacher is that there is no book of rules or teacher's manual to carry about. I am never quite sure what I am going to do when I walk into a classroom—what poetry I will share or how I will begin the class. I am, alas, a creature of moods, and this has served me both positively and negatively. If I am lucky enough to catch the gestalt of the teacher and the pupils, all goes well. If not, we all stumble about for a bit. If this book is nothing else, it is a testament to all that I have learned from the stumblings.

"I learn by going where I have to go," Theodore Roethke wrote in "The Waking." This has been my credo as a teacher.

The first time I was invited to teach creative writing was at the Lamplighter School in Dallas, Texas—a second-grade class. I came prepared. I carefully told the children about the iambus, anapest, trochee, dactyl; threw in an amphibrach or two; and explained monometer, dimeter, trimeter, tetrameter, pentameter, hexameter, and heptameter. I analyzed some well-known poems for them. I insisted that what the children wrote both rhyme and scan. I blush, now, to think about that class. What came to me as "creative writing" was, therefore, rhyme- and meter-perfect, but lacked feeling and imagination.

By the time I reached University Elementary School, I knew what I wanted to do. I was especially eager to work with a fifth-sixth grades class, because during my fourteen years of teaching, from the Dallas Public Library Creative Writing Club through dozens of classes in Texas and California, to my work at the Los Angeles County Museum of Art, the Los Angeles City Schools, the Beverly Hills Public Library, and the Beverly Hills Unified School District, I had never been with a group of children on an intensive day-to-day basis. Thousands of children had passed through my classes, but these groups had met but once a week. This, therefore, was my opportunity to learn something in depth about the creative process in children writing poetry. By observing and working closely with a given group, I could test some of my ideas on a continuing basis. Furthermore, I could discuss the development of these children with other teachers who knew them well.

But for the first time in all these years I suddenly discovered that what I had been doing was based on a nebulous set of principles, values, standards, exercises, and disciplines that I had developed to suit the needs of a given hour. If I felt like reading Walt Whitman or William Blake or Pablo Neruda or A. E. Housman or Lewis Carroll for an hour, I had heretofore done so. If I felt like exploring the limerick or the triolet, or playing a recording of Robert Frost or Dylan Thomas or Richard Wilbur reading some of their poems, or discoursing on the difficulties of writing haiku, I did so. Suddenly, I found that I had to have a plan, and

33

after an initial meeting with Dr. Madeline Hunter, the school principal, in which I explained my feelings about the teaching of creative writing, and a meeting with Mrs. Ann de la Sota, the teacher with whose class I would be working, and Miss Cynthiana Brown, Dr. Hunter's assistant, outlining what I felt was important to get across to the children, I came up with some sort of seemingly reasonable guidelines.

My work would have two goals. First, to develop sensitivity and awareness in each child, individually, and to discover how we could best heighten this sensitivity and awareness. Second, to introduce each child to a variety of poetic forms in which his own feelings could be expressed. It may be that because I am a poet myself, I stress the importance of writing poetry, but I think it goes deeper. I believe that great discipline can be achieved through the writing of poetry—and, as it happened, this proved to be quite true. After the eighteen scheduled classes, both Mrs. de la Sota and Miss Brown noted that some interesting things had happened to the children's prose writing in their regular class routine. They had a better appreciation of the value of words, they wasted fewer words in composition, and they had become intensely aware of the difference between factual statement, classification, and individual feelings. Incidentally, they had all learned something about poetry.

I think it is also important to state, immediately, that in this process not one of us was concerned with producing monumental poetry. When, in all the years I have taught, a fine poem did happen along, well and good. But to make of children's poetry an end in itself, an object of undue praise, is to do a great disservice. I am not concerned with the polished, perfect poem. I am trying to teach young people to express themselves, to know the dignity of individual feeling, to somehow apprehend, if not comprehend, that, as Stephen Spender has put it,

> The reader of a poem has the illusion, through the sensuous use of language, of being in the presence of the event which is the occasion of the poem. The subject of a poem is an event individually experienced; its method (sensuous language) creates the form which is the universal form of all experience for everyone of every event. The reader of a poem is made aware that the experience of every event by every individual is a unique occasion in the universe, and that at the same time this uniqueness is the universal mode of experiencing all events. Poetry makes one realize that one is alone, and complex; and that to be alone is universal.

I do not, of course, read this passage to children, but I do stress time and again the uniqueness of each child, his observations, feelings, and thoughts, in the hope that he will transmit to paper this very uniqueness.

Our first class at University Elementary School began with a stack of poetry books from which I read poems that embodied elements of both formal and free verse. The class was encouraged to go to the library (an excellent one, where I have often read poetry to the children at the invitation of Mrs. Carolyn Horovitz) and check out other books of poetry. I spoke about journals, and a blank book was given to each child for writing in during the weeks of the class. I explained the use of the observation sheet. At this point the children were asked to go outside to an adjoining patio and walk around for ten minutes to observe three to five different objects. Some returned after only a few moments and began to write; others had to be called in. A large percentage wrote easily and quickly. I had established, by the previous reading of work by Langston Hughes, Carl Sandburg, Walt Whitman, Theodore Roethke, W. B. Yeats, A. E. Housman, and T. S. Eliot, that although poetry can rhyme, it does not have to; that we may use elements instead of rhyme—repetition, for example, or metrical patterns —but that the poet's feeling or voice should always be felt. These are the first poems turned in that day:

> The tall, majestic tree
> Embedded in the earth
> Beneath the clear, blue sky.
> *Albert*

> THE FENCE
> The fence is something to behold
> that cages people in.
> if I were a fence maker,
> I wouldn't even begin.
> *Alex*

> There once was a blossoming tree,
>   laughing as hard as can be
> he chuckled and laughed
> 'til he split right in half
> but this wasn't surprising to me.

> There once was a very small bird
>   and his feathers were really absurd;
> they were purple and blue with
> a red spot or two.
> but his sweet song was lovely
> when heard.
> *Alexandra*

THE SKY

The sky is such a pretty thing. A blue thing, a white
thing. An every kind of thing. How free the sky is.
It tells the weather it gives the rain. I will tell you
and once again. The sky is such a pretty thing.

Ami

THE BUTTERFLY
A butterfly flew by
He was very odd
He flew up and down
Not like the bird who soars
But still he flew by
Who?
The butterfly

Beth

In the light of the specific instructions to each child to
use his feelings, we must view Albert's poem as a possible
hangover from some brush with descriptive prose, or haiku.
A "tall, majestic tree" is actually something of a cliché, as
is "clear, blue sky." We are therefore forced to ask at the
outset whether there will be some way of reaching Albert
to draw out his feelings. He obviously has a natural feel for
rhythm and this is all to the good. But, we wonder, will we
ever know what Albert is thinking and feeling?

Alex's poem about the fence shows far more feeling. A
fence becomes a symbol of restraint, "caging in" people.
Alex obviously feels a need for rhyme. It will be interesting
to see what develops in his further writing. I daresay, however, that should the average reader compare Albert's and
Alex's first efforts, he would choose Albert's poem, and
consider it a fine poem. It is about nature, it uses adjectives,

and it suggests beauty with a capital *B*. It is also written with proper punctuation and capitals. For me, however, Alex's effort is far more exciting and filled with promise, for it reveals that Alex has strong feelings about what he sees, and has an eye for the unusual and reacts freshly to it.

Alexandra's two limericks are typical of the first efforts of many children; we suspect she has written them at an earlier time, holding them in memory until needed. For original products of the hour, they are certainly almost rhythm perfect. In any event, they show a good sense of humor. We must reserve judgment and see what Alexandra does next.

The form of Ami's effort lets us know immediately that she has not been exposed to much poetry. It is to be wondered whether her use of repetition is intuitive, or whether she has quickly absorbed my comment, made at the beginning of the hour, that repetition is often used instead of rhyme, for form. Here, again, we reserve judgment. I rather like "It tells the weather it gives the rain," for this makes an animate thing of the sky, and goes a step further than the first statement.

Beth's "The Butterfly" (I am always fascinated by the fact that some children need to have a title before they can proceed with writing, while others ignore titles altogether) uses repetition to a fare-thee-well. I like her comparison of the flying creatures, however perfunctory. It will take a few more poems for us to know whether her feelings can come through.

Cheri wrote three poems.

> The beautiful sun
> Brings light and warmth to the earth
> Joyfully shining

While walking across the playground
I saw little children playing,
Reminding me of the fun that I had
When I was little

The flowers
Blossom in the springtime
Fresh and fragranced

It is evident that Cheri knows about haiku, for her first poem is syllable-perfect. Yet it is anything but a good haiku. I like the second effort far more, for it promises that she can express her feelings. The third has one redeeming virtue, the last word, "fragranced." It will be interesting to see Cheri's future efforts and her growth.

The butterfly flys
so high over our heads, pretty and orange,
He did not stop. No.
But went on fluttering by.
Cherylynne

Buildings tall,
Wide and small,
Flowing, flowing,
Always growing

Higher here,
Lower there.
Older now.
Younger then,
Buildings.
Craig

THE SKY

The sky is blue like the sea.
Birds and insects can fly through it,
like an eagle, or a flea.
It is vast like an ocean,
so it is filled with motion,
because many animals rome,
what they call *their* home.

Dana

Have you ever seen a tree?
It's pretty as can be.
It's nature's way of showing love
Like pretty white doves

They're big and tall
And sometimes small
They're nice
And they intice.
This is the end of the poem I began
So don't cut down the trees of our land.

Elaine

The gully is very calm and peaceful.
It flows smoothly down, with the moss
growing on all sides. The gully is very
calm and peaceful.

Farrel

We can quickly see that Craig, Elaine, and Dana feel that rhyme is a necessity and use it at the expense of sense, in what Hughes Mearns calls an "obstruction of the spirit." Buildings are not "always growing"; animals hardly *roam* in the sky; and if trees do "intice" and nature shows love

"like . . . doves" it would seem to be for the sake of rhyme
alone. It is difficult to predict what Cherylynne will
produce; the verse would be nothing but factual statement
were it not for the "No" in the third line, so the teacher
must suspend judgment and wait to see what will happen
next time. Craig promises a problem; he is not about to re-
veal any feeling. Farrel's effort would seem to be perfunctory, yet we do know that the gully has instilled in her
some sort of quiet mood.

THE SKY

The sky is so nice, up over there, filled with
clouds and no to spare. I wish I was there, up
in the sky with all those clouds, right in the sky. Clouds
are so soft. I wish I was one of them, just as soft.

Fred

I am skating on the
ice. It feels so smooth, clean
and nice. I feel independent and
free and I am skating just me.
I would like to skate some
more but my parents say,
"Come here," with a roar. I
put my skates on the rack
but do not worry ice I'll
be back.

Why, Why, Why the sky?
It reminds me of a ham
sandwich on rye. It reminds me
of love and why. Why
is the sky so high?
Do you know why. I

do not know I wonder why?
The sky is low the sky
is high. I do not know.
Why? Why is the sky so
high?

James

DEDICATED TO THE ORANGE PEEL
Orange peels have many uses,
They're not an unusual thing,
Think about our great orange,
What would it be without an
orange peel?
Look oranges they're pretty on trees,
It's really the orange peel your seeing.

Jamie

A TURNED OVER GARBAGE CAN
A turned over garbage can is'ent
a pretty sight. With all its trash spilled
in delight. let me tell you now if you ever
see, a turned over garbage can you will
agree with me.

Jay

These four efforts represent to me the most healthy beginnings for an introduction to creative writing; they are
certainly not poems, but they are filled with real feelings.
I am not concerned here with poor rhyme as in James's
poems, or lack of structure, as in all the writing, because
what I have here is an honest expression of feeling; and
given that, the forms, the structures, the tools, the abandon-
ment of meaningless rhyme can be taught. I am further

pleased to see that a garbage can and an orange peel are seized upon eagerly as subjects for a poem.

> The ground beneath me,
> Excepting beneath me,
> Due to explode right next to me,
> Run, Go away it will blast very fast, so go from the
> ground
> Take a ship, that partly chipped,
> but when you arrive some where it will still be there.
> Take a rocket, from your pocket, and blast off,
> but when you
> land it will still be there.
> So stay just stay on the ground.
>
> *John I.*

This, too, holds great promise; there is a more sophisticated attempt at inner rhyme here (which, however, is the only ruinous part of the poem).

> FOREST
> A forest has red and Fred your favorite germ
> A many types of worms and bugs
> Thousand types of trees, and bees
> Plants and big ants, that's a forest.
>
> *John S.*

This boy probably has difficulty with ordinary composition writing, and although this is little more than factual statement, "Fred your favorite germ" indicates that there is a voice to be brought out. So here again, we must wait to see what feeling we can elicit from John S.

> A SMALL CORNER
> Makes you want to be alone
> Not inside and not at home.

Makes you want to write a book
or open your eyes, an just look.

Makes you want to sit and stare
To look outside and be glad youre there.

Joyce

SPRING

The world is slowly wakening
Wakening to a new and fresh world
Trees start to bloom
Flowers blossom
And the sky is an everlasting blue
But then, no sooner does it come
      when it is gone
Faded into summer and only memories are left.
Memories that must be remembered until next year.

Julie

SUNSHINE

Like the glow of a candle,
Like the soft rain of a spring day,
Like the sound of a bird chirping
Like feeling love, that's sunshine

Karen

Joyce's poem is one of those puzzlements for a teacher who meets the child in it for the first time. Is it true that Joyce would rather be outside, observing or writing a book, than inside at home? Or did she say these things just for the effect of the rhyme? We shall know more when we see more of her work. Julie's and Karen's poems have a better sense of meter yet do not employ rhyme. Both suggest that feelings are there, yet one feels a necessity to point out to Karen that sunshine is scarcely like the "soft rain of a spring day" and that Julie's "everlasting" blue sky is more fiction than fact. One must wonder about Julie's "memories" and whether Karen would not in actuality respond more in eleven-year-old fashion to sunshine. Are both of these efforts what the children think the teacher wants to hear— or what they really feel? (We shall meet these children again in a later chapter.)

BUILDINGS
Buildings. Buildings. Buildings.
Long and ugly.
Tall and smoggy.

People rushing in rushing out
Rushing everywhere about
Buildings, Buildings, Buildings
Lark Ellen

Here, a sensible rhyme has been employed, but an overuse of repetition and the faulty use of "smoggy," plus a complete lack of voice, destroy the effort. Does the rushing excite or depress? Are all buildings ugly?

THE BLOSSOMING PEAR TREE
A tall tremendous giant,
A tree with a dark, crooked trunk;
Its gay white flowers bring spring
Close, when winters still around.
Lauren

A bouncey place with lots of feet
runing down to meet the ball with a
forward pass and a score for all on
the team with that tall guy they cheer all!
Leeron

45

THE SEAGULL
I am a lively seagull
And I do look like a beagle
But I can't disguise myself
And neither can an elf
But I think it is very legal
Leslie

A TREE
A tree, whose blossoms cover itself,
White, fresh, laughing
Standing, swaying, standing, swaying
Louise

THAT PEAR BLOSSOM TREE
It's tall and beautiful, everything
that is suitable to me.

I like it very much That Pear Blossom
tree; because it is adding something to
natures world. And if every tree could
be like my Pear Blossom Tree, I don't
know what I would do Id be so
happy.
Robin

Our White Tree,
Radiance.
A picture of blue,
Embroidered on satin
Of silken clouds,
With green
And delicate,
Oh,

Spun like gold thread
Shown in small white blooms
Our tree.

Traci

Ever-changing without a purpose
Wandering low and high,
stalking on any surface
as it comes moving by

Lisa

The last poem was not turned in at the end of the hour, for Lisa, a perfectionist by nature, took it home to polish it up. The others were first efforts. The reader is therefore invited to look at these last seven and decide for himself what comments he would make, where the efforts show promise, and where they fall short.

As a teacher trying to introduce creative writing and poetry, how would you respond to the four poems about the blossoming pear tree? Is there a child who shows any feeling about the tree? How? Are the adjectives meaningful or are they just there to impress because the child thinks that many adjectives make poetry? What about the seagull limerick? How does Leeron's verse strike the reader/ teacher? Is he a hopeless case when it comes to creative writing?

Further verses and poems written by this class will be discussed in other chapters. But, as an aside, one might conclude that for children of the fifth and sixth grades, the work, as a whole, is reasonable. A great number of the children have a grasp of how poetry differs from prose in appearance, are already aware of some of the tools of poetry, and have some slight awareness of the possibility of form.

Although I did not comment on the poems at the time, I discussed them with the children in individual conferences. I feel that somewhere in each of these efforts there is something to praise to the child himself, whether it is the feeling, the use of rhyme or the lack of it, the observation, or the mood—or even, if all else fails, the very fact that he has put something down on paper. Whether adult or child, we all need some praise and recognition for an effort made. There is time later to pull apart, criticize, and analyze in a further effort to improve each child's writing.

5: Form Versus No Form

BASIC TO ANY UNDERSTANDING of form versus no form in the teaching of creative writing is some understanding of the different types of poetry being written today. No one has said it better than did X. J. Kennedy in an interview with John Ciardi (*Saturday Review*, May 20, 1972):

> Many poets around the early Sixties got turned off by the old forms. They saw rime and meter as parts of a whole traditional order that they found necessary to reject. They came to associate iambic pentameter with a dead aristocracy and to see open forms as more democratic, more fluid, more honest—more honest, for them, that is.
>
> Just possibly their sense of honesty was affected by the fact that they had not mastered stricter forms to the point of feeling free within them. Certainly such a poet as [Richard] Wilbur feels honest within form and would probably feel dishonest if he broke out of formal containment.
>
> The tendency today is to adulate spontaneity. I wish

the younger writers would ponder what Yeats said about spontaneity in rewriting as well as in writing. I think they do not understand Yeats because they have not let themselves experience containment and the power it can confer.

Ciardi asked:

> Aren't you insisting on a kind of preparation not immediately available to the socially underprivileged who yet have strong feelings and who might never get them expressed if they had first to learn the formalities?

Kennedy replied:

> A poet labors hard and long to prepare himself and finds joy in his labor. Form is his aid. It is important because it tells him, among other things, when his writing is going wrong. When the rime stumbles or the meter starts going ticktock, he is being told that he has shallowed out and that he must go back and make himself feel harder what he is reaching to say. Those untutored and underprivileged you mention will never really learn what they want to say until some sort of form leads them to it.

It might be interesting to equate the "socially underprivileged" of whom Ciardi speaks to the child just introduced to the writing of poetry. He has had no background in poetics, yet he has strong feelings which we are trying to guide into poetry. What, then, is our approach to form versus no form?

I happen to be a believer in the necessity of form if any reasonable poetry is to be produced. However, I think that the child just beginning is stifled by the forms, for the most part, and needs to be led gently to them, once we know that his true feelings are coming out and his sensibilities are developing. If there were nothing else to prove this point, one would have only to read again the poem that provides the title of this book or dozens of examples throughout the book of couplets, quatrains, and limericks. Rhyme, most often, is the culprit here—that same rhyme that is used in the teaching of reading and the English language, and is all too often merely chants and nonsense. Rhyme can be a thing of astounding beauty, if well used, but it can turn its face and ruin the most original of thoughts in the hands of an unpracticed, unskilled child. It is the same with meter. Give a child a set pattern or form *before* he has learned the importance of expressing true feelings, and the results can be disastrous.

The couplets in this poem, for example, are typical:

> Falling asleep
> Soon not a peep
> Not a sound can be heard
> (Unless you become a bird.)
> *Marlene*

One has to wonder what sort of teacher thought this verse about "Dreams" good enough to publish in a grammar school newsletter. It is obvious that whether the subject of dreams was suggested by the instructor or thought of by the child, some preparation in the writing of couplets was introduced, as well as a stress on rhyme. What child would ordinarily think of herself "falling asleep" as not making a "peep"? Would she not rather say something about the process, or where she is, or how it feels to fall asleep? If, indeed, as in the third line, there is no sound (although dreams do often have sounds to them), the leap to the thought of becoming a bird rests clearly on the compulsion felt by the child to rhyme. If questioned, the child would undoubtedly maintain she did think of becoming a bird, but the wise instructor knows better. To truly help this child, one would encourage her to speak further of her dreams: What are your real dreams? Don't you hear sounds when you fall asleep? What sorts of sounds? Are you apt to make peeping sounds? The list of questions or of possibilities for a poem titled "Dreams" is endless, and, in this instance, the attention to the rhyming couplet and metrical pattern has obstructed, if not destroyed, any true feelings and thoughts the child might have had.

On the other hand, many children feel at a complete loss when they first come to writing poems. They are un-schooled in the reading of poetry, have seldom heard it read, and will approach it simply as prose, as a composition. Consider these first efforts turned in by a class of third-, fourth-, and fifth-graders who were asked to write a poem about something meaningful that had happened to them over the Christmas holidays.

THE SOCCER GAME
During vacation I saw a match
A match of the game called soccer.
The first team was Santos.
The color was white

The next team was America
and their maine color was
blue.

Barry

OLLIE AND ME
I have a dog
He is my friend

and he likes to
go for a walk
and bark on
saturday
and when Ollie gets mad
at me he climb over the
fence and scare the cat away
                    Amy

WHAT HAPPENED ON CHRISTMAS
I went to Santa Barbara.
I had a lot of fun.
I got a lot of presantes.
But my favorit one
Is my three speed
bike. My second
favorit one is
a little stuffed rat.
Then I got a quilt and
slept in it all night. . . .
                    Nancy

My worst thing I got for
Christmas was a christmas stocking
and in it a 10 pieces of candy
and a whistle

My best present was a circle
checker game that I never
opened

CHECKERS ANYONE?
                    Scott

Once There was a
boy Bobby was his name
He had a gun and
he shot his shoe
off and then he shot
his shirt off and
one day one boy
came over and shot
his shoe with bobby
but bobby shot it off
and he shot his
toow off too
                    Bobby

We had read poetry for two class sessions before we started writing, and on the day these examples were written, I had begun the class with a reading of Beatrice Schenk de Regnier's *Something Special*. In this book there is both rhymed poetry and free verse. Yet not a child used rhyme in his writing. Barry's first stanza is typical of the child who feels that poetry should have a special diction: "A match of the game called soccer" is not a normal way to phrase these words. There is nothing, ostensibly, in his effort but factual statement, and yet one can sense that soccer is a consuming activity for Barry. Through class discussions we have learned that Amy's dog Ollie is one of her passions. Nancy obviously enjoyed the Christmas holidays. Scott seized on an idea I had mentioned about Dylan Thomas's "useful" and "useless" presents. Bobby's effort is puzzling in light of his comments, during class, about how a Christmas tree symbolizes to him a present from Jesus; I had expected something quite different.

But we are dealing here with children who have **had**

little to do with poetry. What will we do now to make of their statements something closer to poetry?

First, we must work on their feelings. We must find out from Scott why a Christmas stocking, filled with candy and a whistle, was his *worst* present, while a game, still unopened, was his *best*. What is "fun" to Nancy? What are the dog's characteristics? Does he only bark on Saturday? Could Barry describe a particularly exciting play in the soccer game? Is Bobby's story about the shooting off of a toe supposed to be nonsensical, or does it say something deeper about his relationship to a gun?

Next, we must make these children more aware of the elements of poetry, of the forms which it takes. We will suggest that they make a trip to the library and find some books of poetry, choose a poem they like, and bring it to class to share. From these choices we can speak further of the poet's voice, of how he uses rhyme and meter, of how he feels about his subject. Each week we will read more poetry; each week we will write. We hope, by the end of the semester, that we will have been able to come closer to answering John Ciardi's question "How does a poem mean?" for each child, and to revealing how a poem can make of each moment, in Spender's words, a "unique occasion."

We will, in this instance, stress feelings, rather than form, for a bit longer, as opposed to what we might do with the class described in Chapter 3. These children are not as ready as the others for the elements of form—not until we have satisfied ourselves, as teachers, that their true feelings are coming through. And yet, there is a delicate balance. We must not so concentrate on feelings that we neglect to give this group an introduction to the forms. But to introduce form too quickly, before we know that the child has said what is on his mind and in his heart, will further stifle his feelings.

There are no classes, however, in which one can offer a blanket panacea that will meet the needs of individual children. Working with a group over a period of time, one becomes aware of the fact that some children need intensive discipline in sensitivity and feelings, whereas others are ready for form and its elements far more quickly. Some children need both, balanced carefully, and, alas, a few seem entirely hopeless when it comes to growing and developing in either area. I often find that individual conferences with children will work wonders. One must first point out the good features of the work: Yes, you expressed your feelings here, but here I know nothing of how you felt. Your rhyme is good in this instance, but here you have said something you didn't mean or feel and used the rhyme poorly. Rhyme, one continually repeats, is only a tool of poetry. Meter is a tool. Repetition is a tool.

Fred, one of the boys in the class at University Elementary School, started out showing that he had feeling and that he had a slight knowledge that rhyme could be useful. Consider again his first poem, written on February 14th:

> The sky is so nice, up over there, filled with
> clouds and no to spare. I wish I was up there, up
> in the sky with all those clouds, right in the sky. Clouds
> are so soft. I wish I was one of them, just as soft.

Clouds were something he had observed, and he related to them. On the next day, each child was asked to write a poem about winter. This is what Fred turned in:

> Winter is a very cold season, with
> a good reason. Winter almost does it right,
> but not with much light. People always say

that Winter is cold, but why isn't it sold?
if Winter is cold.

My reaction, as a teacher, to Fred's first two efforts, was that rhyme is in the way of his feelings. His observation, in the first poem, that "I wish I was up there. . . . I wish I was one of them" is most promising. After reading the second poem, I decided that we must free Fred from meaningless rhyme and help him put more of his feelings and thoughts into his writing. Rhyme will indeed be an "obstruction of the spirit" in his case.

Following a class session in which I introduced cinquain as a form for possible use, Fred wrote:

> Today
> Today is nice.
> Today is beautiful.
> I wish every day was like this day.
> It's nice.

> Tidepools
> Tidepools are nice
> They have so many animals
> The animals are colorful
> They're nice

By this time I had noted that Fred's observations, in his observation sheets, were perfunctory. His use of the word "nice" (a dull word we had often discussed in class) is meaningless. His cinquains are incorrect syllabically, dull and lifeless as well. Their only plus is that his voice does come through in one line. But the cinquain has not helped Fred a bit—indeed, compared to his first poems, it has stifled his thoughts. As rhyme was something of an obstruction, so is this particular form.

On March 6th the class was asked to write a poem about tidepools, after a field trip.

POEM ABOUT TIDEPOOLS
Tidepools have animals.
Some as beautiful as can be.
Do you like tidepool animals?
Well I do
And I think you do too.

Another perfunctory effort, which, as I explained to Fred during a conference, did not really let me know what he was feeling. By now his observations were a bit more interesting, but I told him that I hardly knew what went on in his mind, and that it certainly didn't come through in his poems. I suggested he work harder. I wanted to know what he liked, what made things "nice," what he disliked, something about his wishes, fears, dreams, feelings, hopes.

On March 14th we wrote "Pretending Poems." Fred turned in two:

THE MINI BIKE
(MINI TRAIL)
I am a mini bike.
People ride me everywhere.
But they feed me gas.
And boy is it good.
People like me because I go fast
But when I go over 50 mph
I get cramps.

THE GREAT SKIER
I'm the world's best skier.
When I race people yell "Go, Go"

> And after the races everyone crowds around
>   me for my autograph.
> Then I eat my lunch
> And boy is it good.
> Now it is time to go home.

One can observe that several things, after a month, are happening to Fred's writing. He has realized that a poem can be written without rhyme; his feelings about things are coming back to the fore. Incidentally, he has also learned that poetry is written in lines. Still and all, we only have a substitution of things being "good" for things being "nice," not much of an improvement, although the fact that in both poems Fred has used "And boy is it good" heightens the use of that phrase a bit. At this point his journal entries are still very much like those of a diary and without much feeling.

A few days later I introduced the class to the limerick. I happen to feel that the limerick is unexcelled for discipline in form and meter and rhyme. Fred was the only person in the class who wrote three:

> There was an old town called Vizes
> Where people were different sizes
>   They woke up in the morn
>   With all their pants torn
> Guess who did it? Tom Trevizes.

> There was a young man from Trevizes
> Whose legs were of different sizes
>   The right one was small
>   And of no use at all
> With the left one he got several prizes.

A boy from Hoboken said "Why
Can't I sit in my lap if I try?"
    He turned round and round
    Till he fell to the ground
And finally gave up with a sigh.

There is something about these limericks that makes me feel Fred has read or heard something like them. The first and second may well be dim recollections of the same original, although the second is undoubtedly more accurate. The third is probably very close to another limerick Fred was trying to remember. This is not an unusual thing to find children doing. In light of what Fred has been doing with his other poems, these seem a little too good, too polished. In a case like this I say nothing, but wait to see whether Fred will write more limericks and how they turn out.

On March 23rd I asked the class to choose something from their journals and write a poem about it. This is Fred's:

POEM ABOUT MY JOURNAL
    I saw something pretty
    I thought it was a kitty
    But it was a mouse
    In a beautiful house.

It will be obvious to the reader that by this time I had introduced the writing of couplets. Fred is now thinking in terms of tighter form. Although this is a poor verse, it does have the advantage of being better contained than his first efforts. Of his own accord, he is beginning to explore the possibilities for better containment and working within the disciplines.

The children had been encouraged, from the first class session on, to turn in extra poems. For the first time, on April 3rd, Fred turned in two:

Couplet: I saw someone ski.
            I wish it were me.

Cinquain: Easter.
            Easter is fun.
            The vacation is fun.
            The candy is very good too.
            Easter.

The couplet is far better than the cinquain, of course, but
Fred has now become aware of the syllable count in the
cinquain, as opposed to his earlier efforts. He is becoming
aware of meter. His rhyme in the couplet makes sense. For
his regular class work, he turned in a limerick:

There was an old town Trevizes
Where people were of different sizes
Where ever they went
Money got spent
. . . .

Fred is still struggling with a limerick on the same theme;
this one poorer metrically than any of the previous three.
The incompletion could connote his difficulties with metrics
and rhyme, but it might also indicate that he is becoming a
better critic of his own work.

On April 3rd I had divided the class, some to work with
rhythm, some with couplets, but Fred was to go outside to
observe and then write in whatever form he wished. Again,
he turned in more than most:

Quatrain: It is a beautiful day.
            Just like the month of May.
            The flowers bloom
            Just like a cocoon.

Cinquain: Flowers
They are graceful
They're very beautiful
They look like red tishue paper
Flowers.

Couplet: I saw some leaves drop
They sounded like a mop

I saw a beautiful bird fly
Way up in the sky

What is fascinating here is that Fred was not requested to work in these forms, but that he *chose* to do them. And what we must applaud in them is the fourth and fifth lines of the cinquain, because suddenly, for the first time, Fred has hit on a poetic image. After all the talking in class about these images, he has (struggling through the inept simile in his quatrain) found one of his own.

On April 6th, in order to see what had happened to each child's growth and development during our class sessions, we asked each child to write about the same subject he had chosen for himself on that first day of class. Fred's assignment was the sky:

The Sky
The sky reminds me about a pool
Shadey and cool
The Sky

Why, Why, Why
Why the sky
The sky is a home
For a lot of animals
Like the fly

> What am I?
> I'm blue
> I'm big
> I'm even a home!
> "Are you the big bad fly?"
> "No I'm the sky."
>
> The sky
> The sky is blue
> It's going to fall!!
> Few———
> The sky

Here, Fred is showing the absorption of a lot of things: a better use of rhyme, an experiment with repetition, simile, metaphor, the idea of the pretending poem, and the idea that anything is subject for a poem (the fly, as well as the sky); but most interesting is the fact that in the last stanza he is unable to finish the line. (The word "Few" would indicate that it is a possible rhyme for "blue".) He is in the midst of struggling with all he has learned, trying to fuse all the elements, the tools, together, still retaining his own voice. He is learning what it takes to write a poem.

The next day was a time assigned for writing about anything the children wanted, as well as a return to writing poems about winter. Fred turned in five poems:

> CLOWN FISH
> A clown fish is
> A clown in the circus doing
> All kinds of tricks when
> He sits down, he
> Makes a big frown
> A Clown Fish

SEA HORSE
A Sea Horse
A Sea Horse is a snake
With a head and tail
He swims slow as a turtle
A Sea Horse

A SEA ANEMONE
A Sea Anemone is a colony of worms
With a big piece of dough
A Sea Anemone

MY WISH
I have lots and lots of wishes
One of them is nice
My wish is for "HAPPINESS"
That's my wish!

FUN
Fun
Fun is fun
I like fun
Don't you?
Fun

Not one of these is a perfect poem, ready for great praise or acclaim, but each shows what has happened to Fred in the course of his growth and development. Contrast these to the earlier poems, in which lack of containment and poor rhyme stood in the way. Fred has chosen repetition as his tool (overused to be sure) and is now experimenting with the substitutions for rhyme. This is a phase that will also pass. Note, too, that Fred is moving toward imagery—not in a subtle way, but through experimentation with simile and metaphor. He is pressed upon by many new ideas about forms, about words, about things observed.

Now, the winter poem which he also turned in:

> Winter is dark
> Winter is a stomach
> Filled with smoke
> Winter

One must contrast this to his first poem about winter, written seven weeks, eighteen classes, earlier, and ask what has happened to Fred. I have chosen his work in this instance not to show what miracles can be wrought (for there were several children in the class who showed much greater improvement), but rather as an example of how a study of form, of metrics and rhyme, on the fifth-sixth grade level can indeed contribute to better poem-making. Fred is not a particularly good writer, but to me he is typical of most children who, given a chance to learn something of poetics, will sift and experiment, feel anguished, and grow.

For, as X. J. Kennedy points out, a poet does labor hard and long, and finds joy in his labor. And form can be an immeasurable aid.

THEODORE ROETHKE asked for a reader who would show both respect and curiosity toward poetry. "Such a reader," he said,

> will not be afraid of a reality that is slightly different from his own: he will be willing to step into another world, even if at times it brings him close to the abyss. He will not be afraid of feeling—and this in spite of the deep-rooted fear of emotion existing today, particularly among the half-alive, for whom emotion, even incorporated into form, becomes a danger, a madness. Poetry is written for the whole man; it sometimes scares those who want to hide from the terrors of existence, from themselves.

There is a delicate balance between the introduction of forms, the elements and disciplines of poetry, and the child's own voice, his feelings and thoughts, which must constantly be borne in mind when one teaches creative writing. It is one thing to wish to help the child make of his words a better poem, and another to interfere with his approach to life. We, as adults and teachers, teach honesty in matters of morals and ethics to our young people, but we are often apt to quash the honesty when it comes to the expression of feelings.

One wonders how many unformed bits or snatches—the germs of poetic expression—lie hidden in the child's mind. They are assuredly there, and sometimes the teacher has the power to bring them out or drown them forever. How many children themselves relegate to the subconscious their thoughts and emotions, because they know, instinctively, that these will not please a teacher? Many teachers pay lip service to the idea that anything is a subject for a poem, yet faced with a frank portrayal of something that does not concern itself with Beauty, Wisdom, and Truth, shy away and pass off the child's thoughts as beneath what they call, subjectively, the "higher" values.

Again and again I go back to an article by a teacher who stated that "Any theme which the teacher feels will lend itself to poetic expression can be used . . . aspects of life important to children like holidays, fire, people, water, the fair," and so forth. "But," she continues, "the teacher must be alive to the possibilities inherent in situations and judge for herself whether or not certain themes are apt for poetry-writing. She must recognize that in some instances poetic interpretation would be unsuitable."

What sort of teacher is this, who, almost *ex cathedra*, can judge what is "suitable" or "unsuitable" for children to turn into poems? While she feigns broadmindedness, she is in actuality making the children in her class toe the line when it comes to writing. She is saying, if *I* feel you are thinking and feeling "right" thoughts, you may write about them. Otherwise, beware! What kind of poetry can come from a classroom such as this? I would suspect that she secretly subscribes to what I call a Sunday School approach to poetry. As long as Beauty, Truth, and Wisdom are personified, or nature is involved, poetry is all right. As long as lovely strings of adjectives or exhortations to virtue are mouthed, all is well. She is undoubtedly the same sort of teacher who expressed horror at Maurice Sendak's Max in *Where the Wild Things Are*, or Mickey in *In the Night Kitchen*, who dared to dream up wild things and get undressed.

If the term "creative writing" conjures up writing of the imagination to some teachers, they wish to be very sure that this imagination is held in proper check. As a corollary, they also wish to ensure that the feelings and thoughts of the students be pristine, orderly, and safe.

Such teachers will elicit the sort of creative writing that does not deserve the name. For it will deal with happy thoughts, the beauty of nature, and joyous happenings, such as the glories of "the fair." But what of the child's depressions, his anxieties, his fears? Are we to pretend that he knows nothing of these and is not influenced by them?

Here again, the needs of the individual child must be taken into account and respected. It is one thing to teach a child that nine times nine equals eighty-one, or that the capital of the United States is Washington, D.C. These are facts, and the answer is either right or wrong. Not so in poetry. What is a unique experience or point of view for one child is not necessarily so for another. I feel that nowhere more than in artistic endeavors such as writing must there be more respect for the individuality of each child.

This, incidentally, also applies to interpreting poetry, as is often done when it is taught in schools today. What has turned more children from poetry than anything else, I have discovered, is a pat interpretation by the teacher of what a poem means. There is no room left for self-discovery, for what George Steiner, in *Language and Silence*, so aptly calls room for "passionate and private digression." Who is to say what a poet meant by a given sentence, a particular image, an experience? In a poem the writer may successfully (and sometimes not so successfully) make his voice heard, but I daresay he would be the first to acknowledge that others may find in it yet another point of view. The poet's voice is not sacrosanct. We may disagree with it, if we like. Further, as a poet, I have discovered that what I have written is often misread, and that questions are asked about poems of mine that even I cannot answer.

Perhaps one of the things with greatest meaning that I have ever read in relation to the teaching of creative writing is a part of a book invaluable for all who wish to teach poetry, *Creative Power* by Hughes Mearns. Mearns speaks of "The Poetry Drawer." This was merely a drawer in his desk into which children could put writing which they did not wish others to see, which was so private that it could be shared only between teacher and child. It is a great testament to Mearns that his poetry drawer was seldom empty. It is an achievement for which all teachers should strive. For it spells out a respect that exists between teacher and child, a bond of understanding. As a peripatetic teacher, I find that a small portfolio or folder does as well. It is understood that when something goes into that folder it is a matter of the deepest importance to the child, something that is too private, too precious to share with classmates. The writing that is put here sometimes stabs the heart, and it is often the finest writing a child does.

Even in the preparation for this book, I have had to refrain from sharing with readers those poems that have found their way into my portfolio or folder. I would be breaking a trust with many children, now adults, whose innermost thoughts and dreams were entrusted to me for a while.

The alert teacher will spot some of these thoughts, even in shared writing. They are often heavily, sometimes thinly, disguised, but they rise up to hit the teacher in the face. Was Joyce, for example, in her poem about the "small corner" telling us that she did not want to be at home, or was it simply a matter of finding a word to rhyme with "alone." Was Julie hinting at certain "memories" that she found too painful to relate?

It was a few years ago, as I recall, that a book of poems by children, written in an inner-city school in New York, was whisked out of circulation by a group who felt offended by what the poems had to say. The poems were anti-Semitic in feeling, and Jews expressed horror. If a book of poems against blacks by conservative whites were published tomorrow, the blacks would protest and perhaps the book would be removed from circulation. Currently, a number of books of poetry written by children stress the evils of the city, its noise, dirt, smog, dope peddlers, and slum conditions. Many of us apparently find it too painful to read about anti-Semitism or black prejudice—both well-known realities—yet will accept the anti-city poems. Most people flock to the "safe" reading of a book like, for example, Richard Lewis's *Miracles*. Here lovely poems about nature abound, a subject we feel is completely safe. How interesting that in the midst of today's turbulent society, given the potential of each child's response to it in poetry, the main emphasis in both writing and publishing seems to be on pleasantries such as are to be found in this book, or on haiku, that bulwark of symbolic nature expression.

There are some children in every group who are willing to share whatever they write. Others are not. It was not surprising to me that after the class at University Elementary School was completed, and Mrs. de la Sota requested that the children turn in their journals, only a few were offered. Most children, in the eight-week period, had learned to cherish the privacy their writing afforded.

These excerpts from Mark's journal, written when he was in the eighth grade, were shared from time to time with a small Extended Day Class in Creative Writing in the Beverly Hills Unified School District:

Nov. 3, Thursday   Today I found out that hate for someone is truly only in the eyes of the beholder. I felt that this boy was conceited, snobbish and a bragging showoff today, while many people were enjoying him immensely. Who is correct, I don't care, and it really doesn't matter. Besides the fact I don't associate with him, I didn't like him in the first place.

Nov. 5, Friday   I saw TO KILL A MOCKINGBIRD. Sometimes I forget that we have racial problems surrounding us, and I forget because they don't directly involve me. This movie made me remember, and made me realize a little more.

Nov. 6, Saturday   At a camp conclave we discussed whether the American Nazi Party should be able to say whatever they want to. I felt that our Constitution gives anybody the freedom of speech and the right to assemble, and we should protect them as we would our own organizations although we don't agree with them.

Nov. 7, Sunday   . . . Being able to be different and disagree is necessary. . . .

Nov. 8, Monday   I love rainy days. Anytime it's cold on the outside I feel warmer on the inside

Nov. 9, Wednesday   The world is in too much of a hurry. Why, even now I have to hurry because it's 10:30 P.M. No matter how independent you want to be people depend on you and you depend on them . . .

Nov. 11, Friday   I crave for the Wild, Wild West. To me it is the most fantastic, amazing enjoyable program on T.V. My brother is wild over the Time Tunnel. (You can see he has poor taste.)

Nov. 12, Saturday   . . . As the snake traps the bird, they had trapped me. First they stuck me next to the most disastrous thing on Earth, a girl. . . .

Nov. 13, Sunday   Saw the Fantastic Voyage . . . One part of the plot deals with the Communists trying to kill a man who had the knowledge both sides wanted. Whoever got it could rule the world. What if the picture was the other way round? Would they show it as we trying to murder the man? Would it be as popular? I think there is a lot of unfair prejudice against Russia, and a thing like this movie can abuse it . . .

Nov. 15, Tuesday   . . . You've got to be a nut to become a teacher but you've got to be an expert to be a great one . . .

Nov. 17, Thursday   There is something very wrong with being labelled. People say that that person is polite and brilliant and that person steals and is sassy. And so we think that one is good, the other's bad. But what if the bad guy started to become a polite, responsible person, and the "good" guy starts to steal, which very often happens. The reformed "bad guy" usually isn't trusted and the new "bad guy" is more than ever looked down upon. People change many times during their lives because the incidents in our lives are not the same.

Labeling causes prejudice such as saying "Look at that Indian boy," or "Look at that pretty Negro woman." Even if you don't feel any prejudice against these people, you are singling them out because of the race. You'd never say "Look at that white man."

Dec. 4, Sunday   Tonight I witnessed my first dramatic play, Incident at Vicci, by Arthur Miller. I considered this play the finest thing that ever happened to me, and was left in a state of amazement because it was so thrilling . . .

Dec. 5, Monday   . . . Maybe people go with the weather. December is a cold, bare month and so are many people . . .

Dec. 6, Tuesday   Is it possible that everything has been written about? People have written on almost everything. There are probably uncovered topics, but one I'm sure of is mud. People think of mud as being dirty, ugly and bad. Nobody's ever given it a compliment. You could say that mud is a gentle, soft sauce that produces beauty and gracefulness . . . Mud is playful . . . mysterious. It's a pig's best friend. . . .

Dec. 9, Friday . . . Being stuffed up with a sore throat makes me think in a fuzzy, unclear fashion . . . I turned on the T.V. Then I see these stupid, ridiculous commercials . . . If Coca-Cola and Ajax really did what they say they can, Russia wouldn't stand a chance . . .

Dec. 12, Monday   The word good is the finest word I know of, although it has become a cliche. All the words that relate to good, such as superb, marvelous, ingenious, amazing, exemplifying, etc. are almost artificial. A good meal or a good grade is honest and blended in. It doesn't tell as much but it's meaning never changes. If you're good you can't be bad at the same time, so good is a good word.

Dec. 14, Wed.   In the subject of history we are studying about the past U.S. History, and I always side with the Indian and have always wanted to be one . . .

Sat.   It's not that hard to tell who is your friend and who isn't. It's the people who like you and the people who don't.

January 25, Wed.   What could be better than cheese cake? (firm but soft, melting, rich taste, lumpy-thick. Never creamy, a feeling of density. A type of dope or dreamy, sensation for taste. Never fills you up, always out.)

Thurs. January 26
I think there is a need for a thorough, good, well put
biography on Will Rogers. Maybe, someday . . . also
General Joseph Joffre!

Although there is nothing here that could not be shared,
many young people would shrink at expressing their feelings about a braggart, prejudice, a teacher, a girl. Not so
Mark, whose first poem shared was entitled "Freedom" and
was written on that "rainy" November 8th.

> I pity the people who don't have it
> Like me.
> I pity the people who don't agree.
> And I pity the people who never
> Do see
> That having it good is mainly being
> Free.
> I can do anything, and much, much more.
> Responsibilities curb my freedoms,
> But life's far from a chore.
> I work to be better, but not for
> Perfection.
> In this energetic world, there's room
> For correction.
> Here, where it's free, we also have wars.
> There's been killing here, and on
>   Foreign shores.
> Why does it happen—why should it be?
> Is this that brave fight for liberty?
> Freedom is costly, it took hundreds
>   Of years
> To establish our rights, and erase
>   Away fears.

Is freedom so precious that millions should die?
Undoubtedly it is, and free men
   Know why.
The Nazis took hold of many minds,
   And crushed the will to live.
Some white men want this for Negro
   People.
This is the prejudice we give.
Will the future contain the faults of
   Today? Or have some peaceful past?
How many chances do we get until
   We're down to our last?
Hate and war grew up as part of our
   Civilization's growth.
World friendship and peace are just out
   Of our reach.
But maybe, someday, we'll have both.

On December 7th, he read a poem about "People":

Around a million years ago we were
   Probably at peace.
Although things were pretty slow,
   Our knowledge would increase.
The lack of knowledge dismissed evil,
   Brought on by advanced war.
The thought of murder had not begun
   Or what hell is for.
The 20th century has begun,
   And men do much for men.
We can fix most wounds from the
   Wars we fight,
But then we're wounded again.

> For countless centuries lives have
>   Been wasted.
> But the biggest waste or wrong,
> Is prejudice, a filthy hate, that's
>   Been active for too long.
> Who knows when this crisis started?
>   But it's there wherever we are,
> In Beverly Hills, in Africa, it's stuck
>   To minds like tar.
> Strip a man of all his rights, slaughter
>   His friends and kin,
> He'll melt away and lose his name,
>   Or revolt and also sin.

It is hoped that the reader will discount the form, the didactic tone, the inferior use of rhyme, and the rambling which marks this early work. Mark was working so constantly with his journal, his observation sheets, and other poems that I felt it important to let his style alone, for a bit. I had suggested to him, however, that rhyme oftentimes seemed to detract from what he wanted to say, and around Christmastime he turned in a perfunctory verse about "The Signs of Christmas" as well as "Mellow Melancholy Miles."

> Mellow Miles lost in dreams.
> Far to go, or so it seems.
> Nothing to lean on, nothing to steal.
> Today has ended, tomorrow's unreal.
> War and hate for when I cry,
> Peace and rest for when I die.
> Mellow Miles lost in dreams,
>   And nowhere left to go.

It should be apparent, from a reading of Mark's journal excerpts and these three poems, that his style is changing;

that he has grasped, through listening to poetry read in class and poems I suggested he read aloud to himself, something about metrics. Rhyme, in this last poem, is used with greater meaning. More important (for our discussion of "The Poetry Drawer"), we can see a shift in tone—here is a boy deeply concerned with hypocrisy, prejudice, war, and freedom, and we can read through the lines and discover that he is growing, and troubled. Asked to turn one of his journal entries into a poem, he began:

> I am a man: I am good,
>> Unlike a tin soldier who sparkles
>> with no reason . . .

The poem ends with the line

> It is a hard struggle to fight God.

Another poem, on pretending, takes as its basis the viewpoint of the writer as a bullet. "A simple mind is far too little prey for me./ I destroy more than men. I deliver pain." The poem ends, "Yet, I would never hurt a dying child." Mark writes about the pain of falling, the race for the governorship, the police as seen from the viewpoint of a Negro, a Bircher, and a bystander; he writes a portrait in verse of a boy called Bob whose "hate is nasty and stings like a rash," and yet "He too is afraid he'll lose that hard toughness." Of hate he writes, using a line entered in his journal to begin,

> Hate is the kindling for a fire called war.
> Its smoke and great heat is past being pretty.
> It filters through your eyes and stays
>> there, leaving pain, as a bee sting
>> would.
> What is smoking, the hate?
> Yes, it's now on fire.

All it took was a match to start
   the fire.
Hate takes deep, angry emotion.
Which is more painful, hate or fire?
Scars from the fire can go away! The pain
   leaves if there isn't any fear.
Hate is fear itself.

By April, Mark had moved away from rhyme. We had
talked of imagery and symbolism in class, of expressing our
thoughts in terms of pictures that would be understood by
all as universals. Here are four poems of that period:

PART OF THE MOON

It left all when it happened.
But I could hear every astronaut/cosmonaut
   cheer in its scoop.
Only I felt it break the oldest crust,
   Harvest its only crop.
Only I? Only I'm not hidden.
Moon men glory.
Yet, I won't share my discovery
   til
You share my joy!

GOD

He made the roses grow so straight—
   blossom the right direction:
   so birds came to sing and bathe.
   Sweet cries—maybe sighing with
      morning breezes.
   Butterflies never flew away from Him—
      not Him.
These were his things. I share Him.

When sick—someone took my pain—put
warmth in its empty hole—maybe Him.
Rockets—buildings—I look for his sunshine.
They grew taller.
Dip your feet in the water. Cold—His too—
soft, warm sand to bury in.
Those were His things. I shared them.
Too long ago. Never again.
Grow— forget the things you own.
Is God dead or have we forgotten
Him?

FINDING SPRING

Too much around my fig tree;
Green it did.
Follow wind for a bullets reach,
No river so long to reach hell;
Tired your world.
Sky—blue enough for suns to show . . . and
smoke—
Stinking your world.
Dust with newest books in old, hot buildings,
Wasting pure rivers your filth in their way.
Valley rang yawning beauty—empty gravel:
Underneath.
Clog around nature—untouchable beauty stepped
On.
I don't know about sky, river and earth
But my fig tree wants to be alone.

On a piece of his own stationery, Mark turned in this:

MY LETTER TO THE WORLD

Dear World,
I mean no offense.

We are separate.

Don't disregard our relationship.
I beg you!
I am.
Stricken in loneliness—unrighteous loner.
I am.

I could easily forget our relationship.
Sinful mock from you happened.
Conceit/ lazy/ unreal.
But not alone.

If you could decide my destiny,
Alas, alone no more, worries!
Predict me—my place!

Only I can speak! Together you are speechless.
Together you killed me: truth.
Yet I live to ask your forgiveness.

One can read into these lines many things: the painful experience of losing one's illusions about good, the fear of growing up to reality. Does Mark speak of himself as full of "Conceit/lazy/unreal"? Is he not "stricken in loneliness"? In this last poem we must read that he is being tortured, fragmented in a personal way, yet he is asking the same questions as eight months earlier.

The next year, as a freshman in high school, he returned to our class. His writing grew more fragmented, more unintelligible. Oftentimes the other children would shake their heads; they could not understand what he was saying. I spoke to him about the importance of all he had to say but explained the necessity for communicating to others. I urged him to read mythology, W. B. Yeats, Theodore Roethke, Rilke's *Letters to a Young Poet*, and to make the return to rhyme.

What kept Mark whole and balanced, I suspect, was an abiding love for the earth, for his garden, for growing things, for signs of life, and a deep belief in his ideals. Occasionally, after he had left the class during his last years in high school, I would see him. Once he wrote me from camp asking, "What is truth?" Always, on these occasions, I would suggest books for him to read, poets to peruse, in which I hoped that he would find he was not alone, that his fears and dreams were shared by others.

A few months ago I heard from Mark again. He had moved to another town and was in college. His draft number had been called up. He was gathering together letters so that he might appeal as a conscientious objector. Reading over his journals, his observation sheets, his poems, I understand that Mark was slated for this. I had sensed it all along.

But I had questions to ask of myself, too. Had I, as a teacher, done all for Mark that I could? Had my insistence on the importance of feelings, Mark's feelings, in any way been repsonsible for a change from ordered, formal expression into the young C.O.? Might it have happened anyway? Did this encouragement to keep a journal, to write, to express himself bode ill or well? I prefer to think that Mark profited from self-expression, from learning to make poems, and that one day he will be a fine writer. He has the potential, for he can learn about forms, about rhyme and meter, and he has deep, deep feelings.

Occasionally one spots in the Poetry Drawer, or in other writing, something that portends trouble. Last year, in a class at the Beverly Hills Public Library, a ten-year-old girl suddenly began writing about nightmares, disasters, and monsters. I felt compelled to call her mother. She had changed, visibly, in class, from a child who shared stories and poems about colors, outings, joyous occasions, into someone who would never volunteer to read or share; in fact, she had ceased to do much writing. Yes, her mother told me, she had been watching newscasts and monster movies on television. I suggested that literature, children's fantasy, might be substituted. I armed her with Lloyd Alexander's Prydain books, with Ursula Le Guin's *The Wizard of Earthsea*, Carol Kendall's books, and Penelope Farmer's, and with a list to continue when she had finished these.

How, the mother asked, did I know so much about the child when I saw her for only an hour a week?

Fortunately, this sort of thing has been an exception for me, but I suspect that many teachers, working in other socioeconomic areas, discover many troubled children through their writing.

The Poetry Drawer. It is there to remind us that we have an obligation to the children we teach, an obligation of respect, each for the other. It is also there to remind us that we can be of immense help, or perhaps that we dare not tread in certain areas of which we know little. Sometimes we must summon the help of others.

> It is a matter of seriousness and emotional risk, a recognition that the teaching of literature, if it can be done at all, is an extraordinarily complex and dangerous business, of knowing that one takes in hand the quick of another human being,

writes George Steiner. Might we not substitute the subject of which we speak, creative writing, and ask the same question?

7: The Collective Poem: Uses and Misuses

ABOUT FIVE YEARS AGO I was invited to attend a class of sixth-, seventh-, and eighth-graders who had been meeting together to do creative writing. I had been told beforehand of the excellence of this group, their high scholastic, as well as creative, achievements, and their unusual ability with words, and I looked forward (in spite of the sixty-mile drive) to one of those visits that might very well teach me a thing or two. Experience, however, had also taught me that what some consider excellence of expression (how many hundreds of book fairs, where "books of poems" written by students have been exhibited, have I seen in my life?) is nothing but a string of adjectives, dull statements, and facts.

My first act, therefore, upon meeting with the class was to suggest that we write a poem together on the board. I had no trouble getting them to do the lines; in fact, it was a rapid-fire performance. My suggestion for a topic met with great approval. We would write about autumn; it was something everybody knew about.

Autumn is a time when leaves all fall
A time to go back to school
The leaves are brown and orange and red
That is the general rule.

Time for pumpkins, turkey and fun,
It comes every year bringing joy and good cheer.
Bundled up children begin to appear.
Halloween will soon be here.

Everyone in the class, including the regular teacher, beamed happily when the poem was written. They were proud of their achievement. They waited, alas, for my praise, and it is at times like this that I would like to produce a broom, pointed hat, and cauldron—for I sense myself turning into an old witch.

"Oh," I remarked casually, looking out the window at the palm trees that grew about the school grounds, "how many of you were born in California?" All hands but one shot up. "And how many of you now living here in California see the brown and orange and red leaves falling in autumn?"

A look of hesitation came on their faces. A few hands went up. One boy volunteered that he did, indeed, see some brown leaves.

"Has anyone seen orange and red leaves?" I asked.

The hands went down.

"I remember," I told them, "that when I lived in the Middle West the leaves turned orange and red, and yellow too, and in Northern California, or up in the mountains, they do also." But, I wondered, here in Southern California in the small community where they lived, if falling leaves of all colors were what autumn was about.

I continued to play the devil's advocate, sensing that the

atmosphere was growing slightly uncomfortable. What did they wear, I asked, in October and November, when they came to school.

"Same thing as I wear now," a girl told me. "A skirt and a blouse and socks and shoes."

"Do you ever wear a sweater?"

"Sometimes."

"Do any of the rest of you," I asked, "wear heavy coats or mufflers or earmuffs or caps?"

One of the boys volunteered that he occasionally wore a pea jacket if the weather was very cold.

"Oh, it's never that cold in the fall," another boy said, while the rest nodded in approval.

"But you told me in the poem that 'Bundled up children begin to appear,' " I said.

Uncomfortable looks passed around.

I turned back to the board and read the poem again. "I am wondering," I asked, "about 'fun.' You tell me that autumn brings pumpkins and turkey. Is there something 'fun' about pumpkins and turkey?"

"It's fun to carve a pumpkin," one girl said.

"It's fun to eat a turkey," another added.

"What other kinds of fun would the autumn bring?" I asked.

The discussion that followed brought out that football was fun, that seeing your friends was fun.

"What about 'joy and good cheer'?" I asked.

"Christmas!" they said in one voice.

I wondered, aloud, if Christmas came in autumn, and when I had learned that it didn't, I further wondered, aloud, if the words "joy and good cheer" meant anything more to them. What *was* joy? And what, indeed, was good cheer?

At last I had them going; each child began to think of

what it was that meant joy and good cheer to him. Allowing a few minutes for this discussion, I went back to the board and reread the poem aloud.

One of the boys thought that perhaps the words "joy and good cheer" ought to be in a poem about winter, instead.

Someone else suggested that perhaps we ought to put the word "Sometimes" before "fall" in the first line.

Someone else thought that perhaps we could take out the orange and red leaves.

Another girl thought that the second line of the second stanza ought to be eliminated. "So should the third line," someone told me.

> Autumn is a time when leaves sometimes fall,
> A time to go back to school.
> The leaves are brown
> That is the general rule.
>
> Time for pumpkins, turkey and fun
> It comes every year
> . . . .
> Halloween will soon be here.

I remember that several suggestions were made to fill in the missing third line, but I was still playing the witch.

"You know," I told them quietly, "when I see a poem I want to hear or see or feel or taste or smell something I've never heard or seen or felt or tasted or smelled before."

They pondered this one.

"But if I have seen or heard it before," I added, "I would like to see it in a new way. You tell me in your poem that in autumn the leaves fall, that school begins, that the leaves are brown, that autumn is a time for pumpkins and turkey and fun, that it comes every year, and that Halloween will soon be here. To tell you the truth I know all this, and I've known it since I was about five years old."

I daresay that at this point I had achieved the pinnacle of unpopularity with the teacher, who looked, I may add, a bit dumbfounded. In ten minutes I had annihilated not only a poem of which she was proud, written by children of whom she was proud, but undoubtedly months and months of work.

"You know," I said, "another interesting thing about poetry is that each word we use should really count and add to what we are saying. Can you find any words in the poem we don't need—space we might use for something more important?"

Bit by bit, we were able to eliminate "is a time" and substitute "In autumn, leaves sometimes fall." Other changes were made, and our poem now read:

> In autumn leaves sometimes fall
> A time to go back to school
> The leaves are brown
> . . . .
> Time for pumpkins, turkey and fun
> . . . .
> . . . .
> Halloween will soon be here.

By now we had lost three whole lines, and what we had left was a minor disaster of a skeleton. By pulling and asking and questioning I was finally able to get the information from the group that this was hardly a poem at all, and really nothing more than a statement of some rather dull facts.

Poetry, John Ciardi tells us, is the language not of classification, but of experience.

Facts, I went on, hardly made a poem, and what was lacking here was the fault of no one present; it was simply that I could hear no one talking, telling me what autumn was about, what made the fun of autumn, or how autumn smelled or looked or felt. Do you think, I asked of the group, that each person might write a poem about autumn, telling me how he feels about it, some experience he has had, something he has seen that might let me see or hear or smell or taste or feel something new?

Needless to say, I have never been invited back to this particular classroom, but I have heard, via a reliable source, that the teacher has never forgotten my visit. I recall the experience now, only to show one way in which a collective poem can be used as a technique to show paucity of imagination, fuzzy thinking, meaningless rhyme, lack of imagery, clichés substituted for words with meaning—in fact, all of the ills that beset the average output of so-called creative writing groups.

It is a valuable technique, used thus, for it cannot help but sharpen the perception of the young people who stumble along thinking in the same old dull clichés, repeating a series of known facts without making of them something personal, using phrases or series of words that are irrelevant and/or serve only as a rhyming device.

A sixth-grade class, under similar circumstances, wrote, just as quickly, the following poem on autumn. (I use seasonal topics more than others for the collective poem, because they bring out the clichés that children, and adults, are wont to use.)

> Autumn's a time when leaves all fall
> We can jump around and play ball,
> And the trees are very barren and tall.
> Autumn is a time of fun for all.

Summer is over and give a Thanksgiving cheer,
It's almost time for the brand new year
And Christmas time is very near.
We have no need to fear.

This poem suited all except one child, who suggested that
we change the third and fourth lines of the second stanza
thusly:

Winter time is very near
And Christmas time is almost here.

In this poem, and in dozens of its sort that I have seen, we
can observe the same sort of dull statement about fun and
leaves and barren trees and Thanksgiving and Christmas.
What the teacher needs also to point out here is the monotony of the rhyme scheme as well. The original fourth line,
"We have no need to fear," is an example of words stuck in
for no other reason than to fill up space. The fourth line
of the first stanza is a typical example of illogical thinking.
Does autumn really bring "fun for all," or might it not bring
sadness or unhappiness to some? We might also ponder, if
faced with such a poem, whether the leaves do *all fall?*
Aren't there trees that keep their leaves—are all trees barren?
I leave it to the reader to ponder for himself how he might
further use this poem as a teaching tool!

I often use the collective poem at the very beginning of
a class or series of classes with older children not only to
show the pitfalls described above, but also to point out that
a poem cannot be written by more than one person, for too
many viewpoints make a poem not a "unique experience"
but usually nothing more than a series of statements. It is
doubtful whether any object viewed, any experience felt,
can be the same for any two people, and this becomes im-

mediately evident to young people at about the sixth-grade
level, certainly from the seventh grade up.

Let us take a look at a poem written by second-graders at
the Emperor School in Temple City, California.

> Bats are flying in the air.
> Witches are scary but I don't care.
>
> Black cats prowl
> Ghosts will howl
> Skeletons will be after you.
>
> Goblins are the frightening ones,
> Vampires are the bloody ones.
>
> Jack O lanterns sit and stare
> Pumpkin patches—beware, take care.
>
> The moon is big and bright
> The sky is shiny black.
>
> The trees make a spooky moon
> Monsters will be coming soon.
>
> Trees look like giant men
> They seem to whisper now and then.
>
> You'll see a lot of trick or treaters
> They really are big eaters.
>
> Halloween brings lots of fun
> But I'll be glad to see the sun.

I had nothing to do with the making of this poem, but I
must commend the teacher who did, for she seems to sense
that rhyme can or cannot be used at the children's discre-
tion. Even if the treaters/eaters rhyme falls a bit harshly on
the ear, it still follows the thought of what is being said.

The only quibble with such an effort is simply that there

are too many viewpoints and one never gets the sense of an individual child looking, smelling, hearing, touching, experiencing the many facets of Halloween. The child who contributed the line "Witches are scary but I don't care" is not necessarily speaking for the child who noted that the "trees make a spooky sound" or who issued the warning "beware, take care." In creative writing we are after the single voice, the child who focuses on the trick-or-treaters, or a gorging of candy, or who might write, as did two third-graders at El Rodeo School:

> I was a mummy
> big and scary, but when
> I looked down
> my shreds were tearing.
> *Adam*

> It was fun
> It was nice
> I liked it so much
> I felt I could explode.
> *Alan*

Though the collective poem, as a poem, is usually a disaster, it can be a valuable learning tool. At the beginning of our third class session at University Elementary School, I asked the children to write a poem about winter. Four children each contributed a line.

> Winter is cold. (Leslie)
> Winter is snowy. (Ami)
> Winter is fun. (Dana)
> Winter is happy. (Alex)

I asked the children how they liked the poem. Joyce suggested that it would be better if it rhymed. Louise thought that by moving the lines around and noting that winter is not always cold and dreary, we would have something better, thus:

> Winter is happy
> Winter is snowy
> Winter is fun
> Winter is cold and dreary

A bit more discussion soon turned our poem into the following:

> Winter is happy
> Winter is snowy
> Winter is fun and snappy
> And winter is cold and blowy.

At this point I inquired how the class liked the poem. Most of the children were satisfied. A few dissented. It was now time for me to ask a few questions: Is winter in California, as the group knew it, cold and blowy and snowy? Alex and Lisa conceded that it matters where you are, that winter can be that way up in the mountains. Lauren argued that winter is often hot. Fred suggested that it is snow that makes you happy and so both adjectives should be left in.

I suggested we leave this poem, for a bit, and try another.

Winter is sometimes cold and sometimes sunny	(Lauren)
In winter you have to go to school	(Karen)
Winter's not summer	(Dana)
It's sometimes fun and sometimes a bummer	(Dana)

Alex immediately wanted to change the second line to

> In winter when you have to go to school it isn't funny.

Cheri suggested that it would be better to write

> Winter isn't summer
> Winter isn't spring
> Winter is everything

but this was rejected by the class. Lauren immediately thought that the second line was poor and should be changed to

> You have to go to school which isn't funny
> (or)
> When it's more fun to be outside when it isn't sunny.

This was also rejected by the class. I called upon John to see what he thought of the poem and he volunteered the information, with Albert's approval, that the third line was too short. At this point, Lauren's hand shot up again, and she told everyone that "a poem doesn't need to rhyme, and that every word should count" (undoubtedly remembering that we had discussed these two points during the first two classes).

Lark Ellen now decided that this poem was nothing but a series of statements and facts. Joyce, Cheri, and Traci agreed with her.

Karen now asked to be heard. It was impossible, she said, for a class to write a poem because each member had his own feelings about winter and had to use his own imagination.

It is at this point that the teacher rejoices and can go into a discussion of the imagination, of imagery. What picture was made in the poem? I asked. None, they all agreed. I asked them what they thought imagery might be.

Karen said that it was "something like something else." Joyce thought it was "how you look at something." Elaine said it was "imagination." Cheri said it was "comparisons." Alex said it was something "that reminds you of something else." Jamie called it a "picture." Leeron said it was "how you feel," and Farrel said it was "telling how it's fun."

As I, myself, have long pondered the reaction that a fine image, used in poetry, produces, I trust the children to know that it is this jumble of definitions, and more, that makes up an image—something that arrests our senses, is seen, heard, and felt, that immediately produces an *understanding*.

A number of things came out of this discussion. A poem is written by an individual and must reflect the feelings, thoughts, and experiences of that individual. Imagery can strengthen these thoughts and become a form of communication—visual, tactile, auditory. A poem is not a statement of facts. It must, in the words of Archibald MacLeish, "call our numbed emotions to life."

I asked the children each to write a poem about winter. To Albert it was the "chill of night"; to Alex, a freezing time for all but "The winter warlock who comes and goes/ and when he comes it freezes toes"; to Alexandra it was a time when "the birds disappear, and the brook's running clear . . ./and all things look glum"; to Ami it was a time that brings "colds to you and me/and the doctor has to come." To Beth, "Cold winter . . ./has his lonely heart buried in the snow"; for Bryan, winter was "Christmas cheer . . . and cold rain." Winter made Cheri "feel gloomy/ The cold wind whips my face," and she relished being in the mountains "sipping hot chocolate and fresh baked cookies." Cherylynne noted that it was a time when "bears go to sleep," as did Craig, whose winter wind was "slowly calling." Dana thought winter fun. Elaine insisted on "snow and sometimes rain." Farrel thought it a "beautiful season" with children "playing in the snowy mountains . . . having snowball fights . . ./making snowmen . . . sledding and ice-skating all day long." James noted that it was a time "for children to catch cold" and have to stay out of school. Jamie liked the rains of winter. Jay noted it as a time to get sick. John I. said it comes "white as white" with a "chill in the air" and a snowman who "comes and goes." John S. talked of sleeping "on a long block of ice" with "Hailstones pounding on the roof . . . the kitchen floor is sticky." Joyce noted it as a time to watch TV while it rained outside. Julie calls it a "dark" and "gray" time, freezing outside. Karen felt it was "gloomy." Lark Ellen thought it "long and weary/cold and dreary" and Lauren "dark and gloomy." Leeron thought of it as "warm soup after and a rainy and cold day with home made cakes and warm pajamas and a good T.V. program to watch." Leslie wrote about "Winter Things"—snowflakes, rain, wind, women wiping the windowpanes—and Lisa wrote of "endless days of frost and cold." Louise thought about the "snow laying on the ground . . . As I sit at the fire on the hearth" and the coming of spring. Robin decided it is "a wheather which things usually don't grow" and Traci offered "For I am alive in summer/Dancing like a flame/Yet in winter/ I become old and lame."

I enumerate these various responses partly to show that, in contrast to the collective poem, there were individual responses to the idea of winter. Furthermore, the forms varied tremendously, the lengths ranging from four to twelve lines, with rhyme sometimes used, sometimes not. The collective poem had served its purpose: as a springboard to the understanding of the necessity for individual feelings. Unlike the situation in many other classes, rhyme seemed less obtrusive, for I had been cautioning against use of meaningless rhyme. In most instances, however, the situation first described in this chapter with the poem on autumn will prevail, and the teacher will have to attack the poor rhyme as well as the other elements.

A collective poem is also a most valuable tool when it comes to teaching a given form, and the meter and rhyme therein. The teaching of the limerick, for example, with its strict form, meter, and rhyme, becomes less a focus on feeling and more on a story that makes sense and yet retains some humor.

It is to be noted that preceding the writing of the collective limericks, we had already read aloud much Lear, and I had introduced the children to metrical feet. For the limerick, the iambus and the anapest were essential, and we had done exercises to find words that were both iambs and anapests. Therefore, the children came to the collective limerick with some preparation.

> There was a young man from Madrid $\smile/\smile\smile/\smile\smile/$
> Who dreamt he was kissing a squid. $\smile/\smile\smile/\smile\smile/$
>   He exclaimed, "Pardon me," $\smile\smile/\smile\smile/$
>   As polite as can be $\smile\smile/\smile\smile/$
> And was sad he dreamed what he did. $\smile\smile/\smile/\smile\smile/$

These lines rattled off the children's tongues easily. I asked for comments. Craig noted that we had better change the last line, as the pattern of an anapest, an iamb, and an anapest did not follow the pattern of iamb, anapest, anapest as in the first and second lines.

Someone suggested we change it to

> And was glad he had only dreamt that he did.

Hands shot up to tell Craig that this would scan incorrectly, and that the word "only" should be eliminated. After much discussion, we noted that with the omission of "only" in the last line, our meter would be perfect.

> And was sad he had dreamed what he did.

But James noted that this change did not really settle anything about the man's feelings. Would he be sad, or rather

> And sick when he thought what he did.

The class then decided that although our rhythm was perfect, the last line lacked real humor if we were thinking of making a funny story of it.

Lisa suggested an alternate line, so that now the limerick read:

> There was a young man from Madrid
> Who dreamt he was kissing a squid,
> He exclaimed, "Pardon me,"
> As polite as can be,
> "I thought I was kissing my kid."

This seemed to satisfy everyone, so we proceeded to another.

> There was an old man of Azoo
> Who wanted to play a kazoo
> But after he tried
> He had it deep-fried
> That silly old man of Azoo.

We eliminated, during the writing, the suggestion that the third and fourth lines read, "But then after he tried/ He soon had it deep fried," because the word "then" contributed nothing and there would be poor metrical emphasis in the fourth line. Someone else suggested that we change the fifth line to read, "And ended up catching the flu," and the class became divided on which line would be best. One student reasoned, rightly, that catching the flu would hardly be the result of having a kazoo deep-fried.

The collective poem can be a way of learning not only metrics and rhyme, but sense as well, as in this instance of a limerick which, again, spewed forth easily from its contributors.

There was an old man from Pippit	(Albert)
Who rode into town on a limpet	(Jay)
When he got into town	(Dana)
He bought a nightgown	(Dana)
And then he decided to rip it.	(Joyce)

Although this was satisfactory to many of the class members, Alexandra was distressed with the third and fourth lines. Acquiring a nightgown, she felt, really had nothing to do with the old man who rode on a limpet, and why not carry through the idea of the limpet by using

> He named him Old Crunch,
> Then ate him for lunch,

Someone agreed that Alexandra's lines were far better, but that the last line would also have to be changed. In the meantime, Louise had discovered that the first line did not scan correctly, so we must make a change from "man" to "person" or "woman." "Person" was the choice of the class.

Our final limerick read:

There was an old person from Pippit	‿/‿‿/‿‿/‿
Who rode into town on a limpet	‿/‿‿/‿‿/‿
He named him Old Crunch,	‿/‿‿/
Then ate him for lunch,	‿/‿‿/
And that was the end of the limpet.	‿/‿‿/‿‿/‿

The fact that Pippit and limpet are not true rhymes apparently bothered none of the children. For the teacher to belabor this point did not seem necessary at the time—too many corrections are apt to discourage children at this age.

Writing collective limericks can be a great deal of fun,

but it is not often done as easily as this. I recall one session in which we had nothing but trouble with one that seemed to scan and followed the rules of rhyme, but had to be abandoned because of a lack of agreement.

> There once was a clown of Sassoon
> Who grossly resembled a goon.
> Said he, in a fright,
> "I'm feeling the light,"
> And that was the end of the goon.

Lines contributed by the class, discarded, and then re-examined for possibilities ranged widely.

There was a clown of Sassoon
> (Two iambs and an anapest did not sound right to their ears.)

There was an old clown of Sassoon
> (Why should he be old? someone asked; it added nothing to the sense of the limerick.)

He looked very much like a baboon.
> (Didn't scan, and clowns do not usually look like baboons; nonsense for no reason.)

Who looked like a baboon
> (Same reasons as above.)

Who acted a lot like a goon
> (How does a goon act? Do we know?)

Who amazingly resembled a baboon
> (Doesn't scan.)

Said he in a fright
I feel the night

(Doesn't scan and doesn't make any sense; what
does "feeling the night" mean to a clown?)

When he got in a spat
With a large Cheshire cat
(What does this have to do with anything?)

When disagreements like these occur, it is often good
to thrash them out, but there are times when it is best to
start afresh. College students or writers of limericks may
well be able to set such a limerick straight, but it is doubtful
that one can hold the interest of a group of fifth- and sixth-
graders long enough to cure all the ills of the clown's situation.

A collective poem can also be useful in explaining the
couplet, the quatrain, the triolet, or any of the more advanced forms. But one should always bear in mind that it is
not an end in itself, but a means by which children can be
taught, and it is *never* the sort of writing we should look
to for the individual voice of "unique experience."

8: When It Is Time for Form and Disciplines

The AFTER-SCHOOL classes and creative writing clubs that I have taught over the years obviously attract the sort of child who finds joy in expressing himself through words, and who is already committed to finding himself through this mode of expression. One usually finds among this group children who are also readers, who have been introduced at home or through a library to literature, and who bear the mark of this reading. Words are exciting to them. They do not need to be prodded into self-expression. Imagery comes easily. It is usually form they are seeking, a better understanding of rhyme and meter and of the way to encompass their perceptions and feelings in poetry that has meaning.

I daresay that given any class of children from second grade on, one can immediately sense the child who has been introduced to literature as opposed to the sort of book that masquerades as literature and that floods the secondhand bookstore or book sale. The commercialism that pervades many book clubs and many publishers' wares, and that produces the flyers that tout "the books your child needs to get into college," has always been an evil against the child. But alas, it will persist, and if we as teachers can steer children away from these books and toward literature, we have been able to perform one small miracle.

For although there is nothing wrong, nothing illegitimate or improper about many books, they do nothing to develop the imagination, the sensitivity, of the openhearted young person.

Contrast the following passages that begin the telling of the story about Thor, in Norse mythology:

1) Long ago, in the early days of the world, the gods of the Norsemen lived in a beautiful city called Asgard.

2) Long long ago in the lands of the North where the winters were dark and icy and the summers brief and bright, a group of powerful gods made their abode. Their dwelling place was called Asgard.

3) Once there was another Sun and another Moon; a different Sun and a different Moon from the ones we see now. Sol was the name of that Sun and Mani was the name of that Moon. But always behind Sol and Mani wolves went, a wolf behind each. The wolves caught on them at last and they devoured Sol and Mani. And then the world was in darkness and cold.

In those times the Gods lived, Odin and Thor, Hodur and Baldur, Tyr and Heimdall, Vidar and

Vali, as well as Loki, the doer of good and the doer of Evil.

There can be no doubt that, although the first and second examples are certainly acceptable prose, the child who reads from the third has been given an additional insight into the beauty of words, the strength of rhythm, and the variations and nuances of cadence. He will come to creative writing with greater potential than the child who has read the other books, and we can recognize that difference in his writing immediately.

For this child we will find introducing form, meter, and rhyme an easy job. He will sense intuitively where his rhythm has gone off, where his rhyme is forced or faulty. We, as teachers, will need nothing more than a sure knowledge of metrical feet and a poetry handbook to prod our memories about various forms, from the simple couplet to the intricate pantoum, and the child can fit his thoughts and feelings into these.

But these children are few and far between, for most of us are dealing not with groups of young people like these, but rather with those who have been fed on lesser books. Therefore, we cannot operate with only a poetry handbook, but must constantly be alert for the point at which a child shows us that he has feelings and is ready to find some form that will best express them.

The progress of Fred, as noted in Chapter 5, was brought about by the use of some simple, elementary forms and disciplines that have always worked well for me. It is possible for any teacher to find among the many forms those that suit the occasion or the student. I do not follow any set pattern in my teaching as to what I will use, but rather let the mood of the class or the individual indicate what may work best.

To the youngest children, one is able to introduce the couplet as it appears in the nursery rhyme:

> One, two,
> Buckle my shoe.
>
> Three, four,
> Shut the door.

It can also be a valuable form for older children who are confused as to the use of rhyme in a poem. For a child like Ami, in the class at University Elementary School, the use of rhyme is confusing. She feels it is necessary to poetry but has no idea how to use it. Our first reaction may be to wean Ami away from rhyme as she uses it here:

Winter has its cold and drear, and also brings rain
and clear. It brings colds to you and me and the doctor
has to cure them one, two three. You wait and wait for
spring, and hear a very distant ring. But still winter
is nice with Christmas cookies full of spice. The snow
is good for sledding. The ice is good for skating. When
everything lays waiting for spring.

Looking at the poem, in better form, we see:

> Winter has its cold and drear,
> And also brings rain and clear.
>
> It brings colds to you and me
> And the doctor has to cure them, one, two, three.
>
> You wait and wait for spring
> And hear a very distant ring.

But still winter is nice
With Christmas cookies full of spice.

It is at this point that Ami becomes confused:

The snow is good for sledding.
The ice is good for skating
When everything lays waiting
for Spring.

Written thus, her verse shows that she is striving for the couplet. Written as follows, the result might be inner rhyme:

The snow is good for sledding.
The ice is good for skating
When everything is waiting for Spring.

It would be impossible to know which of these choices Ami had in mind, but the teacher senses the confusion, and assigning Ami to write couplets may help her, thus:

I met a weaver.
Her name was Sue Leaver.

There was an old man of Levetts
Who always drank Manischewitz.

Here is a cupboard
Of old Mother Hubbard.

There is a man
Who lives in Japan.

It is obvious that the limerick has crept into the second example and that Ami's sense of meter is somewhat lacking. The next step, therefore, might be to assign her special pat-

terns of metrics into which she might put her statements;
for example:

I met an old weaver.   ‿/‿‿/‿
Her name was Sue Leaver. ‿/‿‿/‿

The quatrain is also a form that can be given to children
at an early age. They like the mathematical problem to
solve in the various possibilities of rhyme pattern—*abab,
abcb, abba*, thus:

"How do you like it?"   *a*
"I don't," I said.   *b*
She had a fit   *a*
And turned bright red.   *b*
                    Julie

Look at the chair,   *a*
Look at the ants,   *b*
Uh oh!   *c*
They're attacking my pants. *b*
                    Jamie

I went to a fair   *a*
I was sad   *b*
I was mad   *b*
Because no one would care *a*
                    Farrel

The last quatrain shows a natural step forward into the
need for a study of meter as well as for a greater awareness
of sense. I am not so concerned, however, with all phases
of learning at one time, but rather hope to constantly reiterate the need for feeling, for form, for meter, and for

rhyme with meaning. Here I would simply prefer to praise
Farrel for overcoming the hurdle of rhyme patterns.

Someday, I will tell the children, when what you are saying and feeling, when your form and your meter and rhyme
(or repetition, if you choose), all fall into place, then you
will write a fine poem. But it is not easy. It takes a lot of
work.

The cinquain is another form that can serve as a basis for
putting thoughts into form. Unfortunately, it has fallen into
a great deal of misuse in this country. The cinquain, ac-
cording to Babette Deutsch, is a "form invented by Ade-
laide Crapsey and so called because it consists of five lines,
which are of two, four, six, eight and two syllables re-
spectively." Most of the cinquains written by children
that I have seen in print are nothing more than strings of
adjectives or adverbs modifying a noun or verb, which are
apt to read like a thesaurus and do a great disservice to the
form. I find the cinquain, most commonly written about
nature and beauty or lauding high ideals, a regular bore, but
introduced to a class, with humor prevailing, some amusing
things may result:

> Oh darn!
> My sculpture broke.
> Everything is rotten.
> Nothing ever goes right for me.
> Oh darn!
>
> *Alexandra*

> "Howard!"
> "Howard Coecell?"
> "This is Howard Coecell,
> Speaking to you live from New York.
> We won!"
>
> *Dana*

> Ding, dong,
> Avon calling
> With cosmetics for you
> That will make you so beautiful
> You'll plotz!
>
> *Karen*

Contrast these to the more usual, and far less original, sort of cinquain:

> Silver moon
> Beams glistening
> Nestled in a soft cloud
> Glowing on a sapphire lake
> Peaceful.
>
> *Traci*

The cinquain also serves as a useful example of a pattern of containment. The tools of poetry, I explain to children just beginning to write, are rhyme, meter, repetition, and form, and it is often a puzzlement to decide which tools to use in the making of a poem.

It was amusing to me that a particular poem by Langston Hughes, which I introduced during the first class session at University Elementary School, became a byword among us as an example of repetition. By the time the class was over, every child knew it by heart!

> I loved my friend
> He went away from me.
> That's all there is to say.
> This poem ends
> Soft as it began,
> I loved my friend.

Here repetition takes the place of rhyme, and I watched the many times repetition appeared in the children's work, although we did not focus on it as an exercise. Ami was using repetition to a maddening degree in her early efforts:

> Hamsters
> Hamsters are cute
> Hamsters are cuddly.
> My cat's name is Tabatha.
> Hamsters.
>
> A cat.
> Cats are furry.
> Cats are cuddly too.
> I love cats very much, do you?
> A cat.

Toward the end of the class sessions, when some success had been achieved in purging her of meaningless rhyme and overuse of repetition, she wrote:

> Silly little water spiders
> Flowing down the stream
> Going, going, going, going down
>   the stream,
> And then poof! swimming
>   up the stream again.
>
> Silly, silly things.
> Big and small I like them all.
> They're fun to watch.
> I look with all my might
> To find them day and night
>   Under bushes
>   Under trees
>   Under everything that he sees

> Those silly funny playful
>   water spiders.

Here Ami is still using rhyme as well as repetition, and as
a teacher I must suggest to her that to say that she sees the
spiders day *and* night is not quite truthful and is just further
meaningless rhyme. "Under everything that he sees" might
better read "Under everything that I see." But I will commend her for her repetition of "silly" and "under" as contributing to the thought of the poem. The important thing
is that Ami is growing and is experimenting with the tools
of poetry.

Some children will use repetition to the point of boredom
and must be led away from it. Consider Lark Ellen's first
poem, about buildings, written in February:

> Buildings, Buildings, Buildings,
> Long and ugly.
> Tall and smoggy.
>
> People rushing in rushing out
> Rushing everywhere about
> Buildings, buildings, buildings.

For comparison, the poem on buildings written in April
reads thus:

> Buildings
> Rising up from the ground
> Red brick
> Or dull grey.
>
> Everyone is quiet as mice
> On the inside
> But outside
> Everyone is bustling about to other
>   school buildings.

111

And another poem, written the same week, after observation:

> Along the banks of the clear running creek
> There are trees and plants growing together
> The grass in the water grows tall and high
> To make little homes for the animals passing by.
>
> The water runs clear
> As if it could hear
> The trickle it makes
> So soft and quiet.

Lark Ellen too is experimenting with the need for rhyme, for containment, for feeling, but she has left that earlier singsong, meaningless repetition.

Perhaps one of the most difficult handicaps to overcome in children who do not have an ear for rhythm is the bugaboo of meter. The class at University Elementary School did not experience this difficulty as markedly as other groups with which I have worked, but within the group there were half a dozen who seemed to write to a different drummer. In my experience this is something which the children discover for themselves in their own writing; they become dissatisfied with what they have done and seek guidance. It is then time to employ a technique I have found useful, the introduction of the four most common metrical feet.

I use only four with beginning writers, the iambus, the anapest, the trochee, and the dactyl, and I explain to them that people are oftentimes very similar to these metrical feet.

An iambus ($\smile$/), a weak syllable followed by a strong one, is a fairly steady, usually cheerful sort of fellow who goes along thus:

da *dee* da *dee* da *dee* da *dee* da *dee*

‿ / ‿ / ‿ / ‿ / ‿ /

Depending on the age of the children, we may just all stand up and walk around like iambs (the form of the word they prefer) for a bit.

The anapest (‿‿/), two weak syllables followed by a strong one, is extremely happy and gay; he cannot be sad or lugubrious. Try writing a sad limerick, if you disbelieve this.

da da *dee*   da da *dee*   da da *dee*   da da *dee*

‿ ‿ /   ‿ ‿ /   ‿ ‿ /   ‿ ‿ /

The trochee (/‿) is steady as the iamb, perhaps just a bit more serious.

dee da   *dee* da   *dee* da   *dee* da

/ ‿   / ‿   / ‿   / ‿

But the dactyl (/‿‿) is apt to be extremely serious and, used for any period of time, even a bit gloomy.

dee da da   *dee* da da   *dee* da da   *dee* da da

/ ‿ ‿   / ‿ ‿   / ‿ ‿   / ‿ ‿

The interaction of these metrical feet in poetry is important; anyone who is continually happy and gay, or anyone who is constantly morose, can become dull. Our moods vary. If we use one metrical foot too constantly, our poetry becomes singsong, and none of us are content forever with the nursery rhyme. Here we may stop to beat out, or clap out, the steady beat of "Jack and Jill" or "Mary had a little lamb." This is fine for when we are young, but it will not do as we grow older and our ear becomes more sophisticated. (I tell the children this and their sense of superiority shows in the smile on their faces and the visible rise in their posture.) Yet we cannot defy all metrical patterns, for our very hearts beat in a steady rhythm. We will then try walking in a confused pattern:

da da *dee*   *dee* da   *dee* da   *dee* da   da da *dee*   *dee* da da
⌣ ⌣ /   / ⌣   / ⌣   / ⌣   ⌣ ⌣ /   / ⌣ ⌣

For those children who read music, one can also draw a series of irregular and incorrect measures and notes on the board, or try singing a song with incorrect values assigned to the notes. It does not take even the dullest child very long to appreciate what rhythm means in terms of movement. A series of sentences, jerkily delivered, will also get across the message.

A great majority of children sense all this instantly, yet there always remain a few who find it difficult. For those children, the limerick can be most helpful—for the discipline of its lines must conform, each to each. I have discovered, however, another form invented by Edward Lear that can work miracles in this regard.

Teapots and Quails   /⌣ ⌣/
Snuffers and Snails   /⌣ ⌣/
Set him a sailing   /⌣⌣ /⌣
And see how he sails!   ⌣/ ⌣⌣/

Here we are using the four feet, rather mixed up, but we are not using them as a mere exercise in metrical feet (reserved for older children), but with the nonsensical delight of naming things as well as finding rhymes:

Watches and Clocks
Latches and Locks
Set it a tocking
And see how it tocks.
Bryan

Coffins and Sighs,
Founders and flies,
Set it a dying
And see how it dies.
Farrel

A reading of verses from *Teapots and Quails* has stimulated most children I know, and helps immeasurably with meter.

For the more advanced child, the triolet can be a happy experience with form. I have seen hundreds that express everything from being a rubber band, to a hatred of smog or cauliflower, to the parody of the triolet I use to introduce the form, "The Kiss" by Austin Dobson.

> Rose kissed me to-day.
> > Will she kiss me to-morrow?
> Let it be as it may,
> > Rose kissed me *today;*
> But the pleasure gives way
> To a savor of sorrow;
> Rose kissed me to-day;
> > *Will* she kiss me to-morrow?

> Paul bit me today.
> > Will he bite me tomorrow?
> No skin there does lay.
> Paul bit me today
> But the terror gives way
> > To pleasure, not sorrow.
> Paul bit me today.
> > I will bite him tomorrow.
> > > *Susan*

For a seventh-grade child like Susan many forms are possible, and parodies are not only fun to do, but provide the discipline of set patterns and rhyming schemes. A parody of "Jingle Bells" turns out to be:

> Dashing through the streets
> In a bashed-up Chevrolet
> Through the smog we go

Choking all the way.
Brakes on autos screech
Making people pray.
Oh, what fun it is to live
In down-own-town L.A.

(Chorus) Smog and soot, smog and soot,
Air pollution's here.
How grand to have the blackened skies
To greet the brand New Year.

Lisa

The beginning writer's parody may be much less complicated, but the message gets through:

Roses are red.
Violets are blue.
But now there's pollution
And this isn't true.

Karen

Introducing many forms can help a child find that sort of expression to which he is best suited. The tercet, villanelle, rondel, and rondeau all offer possibilities to children who have mastered the basic, simple forms. I remember Edwin, who wished to say something of his boredom at watching television, and expressed this in couplets, limericks, triolets, quatrains, and even sonnets! I was reluctant to give the sonnet to an eighth-grader, for I usually avoid it at this age. But Edwin was deliriously happy with his.

Another of the forms that I use frequently is the ballad. It has the advantage of telling a story (which children like to do) and can either adhere to or depart from rhyme. The ballad literature available to us in anthologies allows each of us teachers to choose what would seem most meaningful to us, as well as to the particular group of children with whom we come in contact. From "Lord Randal" and "Sir Patrick Spens" to "Frankie and Johnny" and the ballads of Woody Guthrie and Bob Dylan—the choice is wide. Ballads written by the children can focus on someone they may be studying in a social studies or history class. My favorite method is to ask them to watch the newspapers or magazines for a story that can be turned into a ballad. For some it is more fun to make up a character about whom to write.

> His days were numbered.
> That much I know.
> He robbed all the stores and
> Took all the dough.
>
> One day at the beach club
> He was doing his thing.
> He took diamond necklaces,
> Bracelets, rings.
>
> The cops came up quickly
> Before he could run.
> They pulled out their rifles
> Revolvers and guns.
>
> They told him to stop
> But he ran on and on.
> So they shot at his legs
> And he fell like a bomb.
>
> He fought like a tiger
> But he knew he couldn't win.
> His hands were in cuffs
> And he cursed like sin.

They clapped him in jail
And his trial came soon.
His career was in ruin.
He was Chester McGoon.

The day that they hanged him
Was a day for them all.
People were cheering
And were having a ball.

Chester's son, Marvin,
Was chasin' the fad.
He followed the footsteps
Of his dear old dad.

His days were numbered.
That much I know.
He robbed all the stores and
Took all their dough.
                    Lisa

For an eighth-grader like Lisa, it is also a challenge to turn
to the French ballade, whose charm depends on the envoi
and the discipline of using three rhymes only, with the
refrain repeated, as below:

The sewers drop waste in the sea.
The smokestacks pour smog in the sky.
The cars go as fast as you see
And the birds are too frightened to fly.
Tears flow from each sore tired eye.
All lungs are as flimsy as tape.
All men have announced with a cry
        "The world is in terrible shape."

Scientists research cures—for a fee.
Poor people barely get by.

The Pres has the brain of a pea
(Although he's a really nice guy).
The workers all give a great sigh
As prices and wages do gape,
And people are wondering why
      The world is in terrible shape.

The people have ended their glee
For all will soon go out and die.
There is no single flower or tree
That the sun may endeavor to fry.
No more will people say "Hi"
Not even a roll of orange crepe
Is left to be shocked and say "My,
      The world is in terrible shape."
      (*Envoi*)

Dear President, please do not lie!
Don't strangle us all in red tape.
But simply agree and say "Aye,
      The world is in terrible shape."

In spite of the imperfections of this ballade, the form can be a challenge to the talented child who has gone beyond the early disciplines of couplet, quatrain, limerick, and cinquain. And yet, the teacher must always come back to these, always insist that within the simplest couplet lies potentiality for expression.

      Spring is a run around
      Of coils tightly wound.
          Susan

9: Metaphor and Simile: When and How?

WE HAVE BEEN speaking of many things in the fore-going chapters, from the blank piece of paper that stares at the child about to express himself to the teacher's obligation to that child in helping him achieve that expression. We have touched on the goals we have in mind, to develop the child's sensitivity by introducing him to the disciplines of observation and journal writing and to help him find forms in which he can express his feelings.

At the same time we are working toward putting an end to meaningless rhyme, teaching the child something of meter, and introducing other elements that may help him to function. We are reaching for his thoughts, respecting their privacy, if needed, but encouraging him to communicate them to others. We are teaching the discipline of what Robert Frost calls "the best words in the best order" and stressing that the clichés of the world do not belong in good poetry. We are using both the collective poem and the individual's effort to point out inadequacies, yet at the same time praising the strengths of each contribution.

Up to this point, stressing experience and observation, we have circumvented that warhorse of poetic expression, the metaphor or the closely related simile. I daresay that a large percentage of the creative writing done in most classes *begins* with this sort of emphasis, and it is indeed time to explain why I have avoided it just as strenuously as many teachers stress it.

The fact is that the unskilled child, just beginning to write, is perfectly capable of understanding how one thing can be compared to another and can list any number of things that "remind me" of other things. Unfortunately, these metaphors and similes are often used as an end product, rather than a means, and are merely illustrative, rather than contributing to the making of a poem. A good metaphor or simile should be functional. For too long, children have written meaningless lists of similes and metaphors and been praised highly for their observations and perceptions. Thus:

> Our White Tree,
> Radiance.
> A picture of blue,
> Embroidered on satin
> Of silken clouds,
> With green
> And delicate,
> Oh,
> Spun like gold thread
> Shown in small white blooms
> Our tree.
> *Traci*

> Like the glow of a candle,
> Like the soft rain of a spring day,

Like the sound of a bird chirping
Like feeling love, that's sunshine
Karen

Ladybugs
Ladybugs tickle
When they're on you
They remind me of four leaf clovers.
Fred

Winter is the chill of night
When we bundle in our beds
Winter is a snowball fight
When we meet the first snowman
Albert

In Traci's poem it is difficult to know what is "spun like gold thread," even when one observes the blossoming pear tree. Lofty adjectives cover up the potential feelings in the writer, and the simile is completely meaningless. To say that sunshine, in Karen's poem, is like the glow of a candle or the soft rain of a spring day, or the sound of a bird chirping, or feeling love, may initially strike the reader as interesting, but the poem is merely a series of classifications. It is one thing to chuckle at Linus's definition of happiness as a warm puppy and similar metaphors, but let us not fool ourselves into thinking that this is the stuff of good poetry. This sort of listing is evident again in Albert's poem, and doesn't Fred's comparison of ladybugs to four-leaf clovers strike one as a bit far-fetched?

Metaphor is used to suggest both comparison of one object to another and, in many instances, differences as well. A good metaphor will serve as a springboard; it will be functional and allow the poet to further express his feelings or thoughts in keeping with the striking comparisons or differences. Thus, we have the "aged man" of W. B. Yeats, who is "but a paltry thing,/A tattered coat upon a stick, unless/Soul clap its hands and sing, and louder sing/For every tatter in its mortal dress"; Andrei Voznesensky's bicycles—"Petrified monsters/Their chains entwined./Huge and surprised/They stare at the sky"; and Shakespeare's "All the world's a stage," with its extended images. Simile, more easily recognizable by the use of "like" or "as," is usually more sterile, for it merely joins two separate objects. Juan Ramón Jiménez tells us that "Time will fly ahead of you like a/Fleeing butterfly" and, "Time will walk behind you/Like a submissive ox." Yeats's old men "had hands like claws, and their knees/Were twisted like the old thorn-trees."

Children do write many poems with fresh looks. "Tell me something new, something I have never known or seen or tasted or smelled or touched or heard before," I say to the children. "Or, if you do not know something new, tell me something old in a new way—your way!" I am, of course, hopeful that, from this, metaphorical writing may ensue, but I am loath to make of metaphors and similes a fruitless exercise.

The same Fred who wrote about ladybugs reminding him of four-leaf clovers also wrote:

> Leaves are green
> Some leaves are tall
> When they blow with the wind
> It sounds like popcorn popping.
>
> White clouds
> They move like turtles
> They're all over
> White clouds

The lines about leaves were, unfortunately, imitative of a classmate's visual observation, but Fred's observation about clouds as turtles shows possibility. Again, unfortunately, the line "They're all over" does nothing to further the striking quality of the observation, and the total poem, while it shows growth in Fred, leaves us unfulfilled.

Far more promising than any of the lines given above, though less skilled in form, is the effort of a third-grader at Fairburn Avenue School who wrote about "The Jungle Gym."

> I wonder how the jungle gym
> got so many arms,
> Maybe it grows them.
> The jungle gym makes me
> think of a monster.
> I think the bar in the middle
> Is where his food goes down.
> *Patty*

For a first poem by a third-grader, this shows unusual promise in the making of metaphor.

After the eighth class session at University Elementary School, I asked the children to work, over a weekend, on a poem about tide pools. A trip the class had taken to the beach, an aquarium in the classroom, and the children's keen interest in sea life and ecology suggested to me that this subject would be of interest to all; furthermore, John had turned in an "extra" poem on the tide pools (to be discussed in Chapter 10).

Two classes later, with the tide pool poems in hand, I decided to read from the nineteen poems turned in.

> Many times I've been to the tidepools.
> Many times I've seen crabs, lobsters and snails.

Many times I've smelled ocean air.
And I've always been happy
At the tidepools.

Alex

The class immediately recognized that Alex had used repetition, rather than rhyme, to bind his poem together. If a few noted that this was not much more than a listing of things seen and smelled, a few others noted that at least he had put in his thoughts about being "happy." Cheri wrote,

The tidepools are fasenating
All the sea animals crawling around
They make me feel lonely
Because they're lonely
Everything's dark, frightening and a tragedy.

Some thought it was good that Cheri expressed her feelings about being lonely. When pressed for an explanation of the "tragedy," Cheri told us that it was indeed a tragedy that people carried off specimens from the tide pools and dropped litter on the beaches. This point had been reflected in many other poems, for example:

The tidepools are nice
with lots of life
So don't spoil it
By taking things.
John S.

This poem is a perfect example of the preaching or didactic poem, and it is well to point out to students that poetry is not meant to instruct others so directly, but rather to present a point of view that others may accept or reject.

When I go to the tidepools
I don't take away
Any of the animals who live there.
They're interesting to watch
And I love to pick them up
But I'm always sure to put them back.

Lauren

James had put his tide pool poem into a cinquain (faulty in the third line, as noted by all).

Tide pool
is very still
Suddenly something moves about
A few animals move about
Silent.

Lisa had used repetition:

The tidepools are an
    ever changing place
Changed by the tide
Are the nooks and crannies
with an anemone,
a sea star,
or even a crab within.
An ever changing place
Changed by the tide.

The last poem I read was written by Julie:

TIDEPOOL SUBURBS
Safe in the tidepool suburbs
Away from the ocean's roar,
See the crab commuters
Hurrying to and fro.

See the sea urchin housewives
Cleaning the tidepool floor,
While pink anemone maidens
Wave tentacles
Flirting with opaleyed fish,
Slowly passing by.

See the aged barnacle ladies
Sit and gossip all day,
And baby squid play hide and seek
Around and around the rocks.

> It's low tide time in the suburbs
> The start of another day
> It'll go on, 'till the tide comes in
> And then, splash, the day ends.

It would be difficult to describe the state of the classroom when I had finished reading this poem. It came to life with "oh's" and "ah's" and spontaneous applause. A few mouths even fell open. A revelation had occurred.

There will always be one Julie in every class, who opens up the world of relationships and comparisons, the world of metaphor with meaning for the others. And I maintain that no amount of exercises in metaphor or simile can mean as much as waiting for just one child to point the way.

It was interesting to me to make some comparisons of my own a week later, when I again assigned the tide pool as a subject for a poem. The work of three children is notable for the change that had occurred in their way of looking at things.

First Poem 3/6	*Second Poem 3/14*
TIDEPOOLS	BARNACLES
The tidepools are	Closed up in their shells,
wonderful and fascinating	Hiding from the world

127

To your eyes.
　You look everywhere
And everything is beautiful
Around you.

Warm and cuddly in their
　houses,
　Lonely barnacles

Farrel

Tidepools are full of life
Because man hasn't invaded it

Little hermits look
Like popcorn popping

Small fish flash
Like lightning

Sea Stars like
Stars in the sky

They all make a
Tidepool

Jamie

THE SEA ANEMONE

I have no feeling for the
　tidepools
They really don't mean much
Except for oceanography
To me it seems much more
　interesting

The sea anemone sits
Looking like a regal queen
Wearing an Elizabethan collar
Staying there so serene

All of a sudden the tide goes
　out
And the queen closes herself
Locking out the dryness
And looking no bigger than
　the
Ball of an elf.

Louise

At the third-grade level, this same thing happens in interesting ways and is ever a source of surprise to the instructor. Consider the class at El Rodeo School, on the first day back from Christmas vacation. We had taken as our point of observation a Christmas tree and had written on the board all the facts we could think of. A Christmas tree could be green, or flocked, or pink, or blue—almost any color. It has branches. It is usually a pine tree. It has ornaments. It has lights. It can be any size. One girl who suggested it is "lovely" was immediately corrected by a classmate; it might be "lovely" to her, but to another it was not. Therefore, we started our left-hand column by listing all of the various subjective responses the children had to the tree. It was beautiful and colorful; it made this one feel happy and that one feel excited and another feel like singing Christmas carols. It made another think of getting presents and another of wrapping presents to give.

This done, paper was passed out and the children were asked to write a poem about a tree or a present or any trip they had taken over the holiday. A previous class session had established the fact that a poem is not facts alone but is filled with feeling. Nevertheless, with a myriad of possibilities to choose from, two or three children could think of nothing to put into a poem. Susie, in particular, was frustrated over how to begin. She knew what she would like to write about—a large candy cane her brother had given her for Christmas. After ten minutes she had written, prose-fashion, on a sheet of pink colored paper,

> My brother gave me a 3
> foot candy cane and it is
> 3 inches wide.

"It's nothing like a poem," she wailed.

I suggested that everyone stop his writing and try to help her.

So we started on the blackboard, listing all the facts about the candy cane. I drew a picture of it, three feet tall and three inches wide. We wrote down these facts: It was striped. It was red, white, and green. It was wrapped in cellophane. It was made of sugar. It tasted sweet (it did not taste like meat loaf, for example). Then, we started the left-hand column: I like it because my brother gave it to me. It will last a long time. It will last me until next New Year's Eve. "Would you share it?" I asked. "Oh, yes," Susie answered. "I would bring it to school and give everyone a piece." "What would happen," I asked, "if you gave everyone a piece and had nothing left for yourself?" "Oh, it's so big I would have some left, and if I didn't, my brother would buy me another one."

I explained to Susie and the class, at this point, that now she had more ways to begin her poem; she could start at any one of ten or twelve points we had written down. Then, quite deliberately, and feigning absent-mindedness, I began to draw more candy canes, some upside down, some in pairs. One boy interrupted me.

"You know what I think about the candy cane?" Brian said. "When I lived in New York and went to Grand Central Station I saw a train that looks like the candy cane. If you put it on its side with the round part up, it's like one of the trains."

I obliged him, but before I had finished drawing, another child likened the horizontal candy cane to a ski, another insisted that I draw one at a forty-five-degree angle that made of it a ski jump, others chimed in and discovered that in pairs candy canes looked like a reindeer's antlers. A cane became the letter "J," the tail of a tiger or squirrel, a sea serpent rearing from the water. Every class member chimed in with some sort of comparison.

This, too, can be a beginning or a kind of beginning for the discovery of simile, but I noted that on my next visit to the class not one of the children carried the remembrance of that discovery even though I asked about the candy cane and found that, indeed, Susie had brought a piece to each child.

On this particular day, three weeks later, I had brought poems to read about frogs: Hilaire Belloc's "Be kind and tender to the frog/ And do not call him names"; the old nursery rhyme "Frog, he would a wooing go," the children chiming in on the chorus; the anonymous "What a wonderful bird the frog are"; and Stella Gibbons's "Lullaby for a Baby Toad." I had also done something I seldom do, employed the visual aid of a photograph of three frogs in full color. My suggestion that we write poems about frogs was met with detailed descriptions of frogs, stories about frogs, children pretending they were frogs. What, I asked myself, would Bryan, the boy who had started us off on comparisons of candy canes, write? This was it:

> Thumpy, Dumpy and Sam
> Lived with a man,
> brother, sister and brother.
> They have no father or mother.
> They are funny, funny.
> They remind me of a bunny
> Because they are so funny.

The point is where do we as teachers go from here? Do we decide that on the next visit to the class (in my case) or in the next session on creative writing we will go back and find an object that can be thought of in terms of simile or metaphor? Will we devise an exercise that will pinpoint "it reminds me of" or "it is," or will we rather wait to see what occurs—wait for Bryan or another child to write something that we can share as a contrast or comparison of two objects, two thoughts?

I am not a purveyor of magic pills, nor of set patterns of teaching that will ensure brilliant metaphorical writing. I believe that we can gently guide, seizing the time, as it were, when a Julie or a Bryan leads the way, but I would rather wait for the moment and let a peer lead the children to new ways of thinking and expression. It is the growth of the child's mind with which I am most concerned, and a belief that if metaphorical writing comes naturally, well and good. Otherwise, we must wait patiently.

10: Rhyme: A Double-Edged Sword

DONNA, A THIRD-GRADER, likes to write poetry. She likes it so much that she turns in a small booklet of her own poems, dwarfing the contributions of the other children in her class.

> I like love
> And I have a dove
> do you have a mouse
> If you don't have a mouse
> I have a house.
>
> I think love is nice
> And so are mice.
> I like my Grama
> And Alabama.
> I like my spice
> And so does my mice.
> and my ice.
> and my dice.

Three variations on this poem add that "I like you/Because you are taking me to the zoo." Another reads:

WHAT I LIKE
I like girls and boy.
Do you know why
I like boy because I like toy.
I like balls and sometimes
I like dolls.
but do you know who
I relly like my mom and
dad. when he is sad
Im mad
you're very nice
nicer than my spice.

Asked to write a Halloween poem, Donna turned this in:

I saw a house.
It had a mouse
She is nice
and so is her spice
that she puts in her pot
but the pot is so hot
I like the house
it has a pointed roof
and so does my tooth.
I had fun
and so did her son
I had a doll
and my brother
had a ball.
She had a bat
and a cat.

Asked to write a poem that does not rhyme, Donna whines and begs permission to use rhyme. "Why can't I use it?"

she asks. "Because you don't tell me about your feelings or thoughts," I answer. Donna obliges by not writing anything.

This may sound like an extreme case, but it well portrays the approach of many children to poetry. If it doesn't rhyme it isn't a poem, and no amount of reading free or blank verse, which may or may not use repetition or other forms of pattern structure, will free them from this senseless use of rhyming words.

The patience of the teacher, under such circumstances, can often be tried to the breaking point. What is there, one asks, in the school reading program, the primers, or the other sorts of reading these children do that necessitates this insistence on rhyming words at the expense of all sense?

I have read so many "poems" about a cat in a hat with a bat who is fat that I am sure more children are familiar with Dr. Seuss's *The Cat in the Hat* than any other book in its field. I often wish that teachers and parents would familiarize themselves with *And to Think That I Saw It on Mulberry Street* instead. I am worried that an overdose of Dr. Seuss's imitators has done a great disservice to the potential for real poetry, for, unfortunately, most children know this sort of work as the only poetry and/or verse with which they come in contact. When there isn't a book of poetry in a child's home, the teacher must (in addition to a thousand and one other duties) serve as a mentor in helping him cultivate a taste for real poetry: poetry (not merely a story told in verse) that has meaning and offers some look into a "unique occasion in the universe."

Meanwhile, we must meet the Donnas as best we can, asking patiently whether Donna really has a dove and a "Grama," and why she likes Alabama (the chances are she doesn't even know what it is) and whether she has dice, and does she really get *mad* if her father is sad, and does her tooth really have a roof, and whose son is she speaking of? Slowly, slowly, we may be able to help her grow. But the growing is often painful for both student and teacher.

Many children will defend their rhymes, insisting on their right to use what they first thought of, no matter how senseless, and maintaining that the rhyme scheme must be left as it is. I am reminded of the day John I. turned in an "extra" poem on the tide pools. The next day in class I read it to the others for three reasons: first, to show that poetry should not preach. "The reader has intelligence," I told the class, "and you must not exhort him to certain kinds of behavior. Let whoever is reading your poem know, from your images or thoughts or feelings, how you feel about something; perhaps he will feel the same way too, or it will lead him to know that your experience has something to say to him too." Secondly, I used the poem as a springboard for showing how mere statement of fact dominated the poem. But thirdly, I wished to point out how insistence upon rhyme can ruin the thought.

> The tide pools are a place to look
> A place where you won't get a rook
> They have snails, starfish and crabs,
> But they shouldn't be hurt
> Killed or be grabbed.
> The tidepools are a fun place to go
> But all you should leave is the
> Mark of your toe.

I first explained my puzzlement over the word "rook" in the second line. The rook as I knew it, I told John, was a European crow. No, he told me, he had never even heard of a rook that was a bird. I also knew, I told him, of the rook in the game of chess, but I doubted that he would ever look for one at the tide pools.

Several boys laughed outright. Who was this uninformed teacher who didn't know that if you were "rooked" you were cheated? John shook his head positively. *That* was the kind of "rook" he meant—like when you go to certain tourist places you get cheated and the money you spend isn't well spent. John meant that in going to the tide pools you wouldn't get cheated. I further suggested that if this was what he really meant, perhaps he should say "A place where you won't get rooked." To "get a rook" means literally to get a swindler or cheat. No, he said, he didn't mean that either. "Then," I asked, "may we change it to the sentence I suggested?" "No," he held firmly, "it wouldn't be the right rhyme that way."

There was some discussion among the class members as to whether one would actually think of being cheated at the tide pools, or whether one could say something more important about them in the second line. But John, again, was adamant. He had said what he wanted to say. We went on, therefore, to the last three lines. One student pointed out that "a fun place to go" could be better expressed, but John held firm. Therefore, I again innocently inquired what "mark of your toe" meant. "Oh, you know, Mrs. Livingston," a number of children piped up, "like a footprint in the sand." A footprint, yes, I knew about that. I had seen many footprints in the sand—of birds and horses and dogs as well as people. But never had I seen, in all my wanderings over the beaches, the "mark of a toe." How could this be made? I suggested we all stand up and demonstrate how one could leave a single toeprint. We did. "You just put your toe in the sand and then hop away." "But," I persisted, "you can't just hop along on one toe, and

John has told us that is *all* you would leave. It simply isn't physically possible."

I recall that two of the girls were extremely defensive, at this point. The old witch was indeed on her broomstick, and they were protecting John. John did not, as I remember, budge an inch. The poem had to stand as written, although I could sense in the boy a certain puzzlement.

Looking back to the first lines John had written, I knew that rhyme was nothing he felt absolutely necessary to a poem. Indeed, he had avoided end-rhyme entirely, and used instead, in a most creative way, the inner rhyme of "it will blast very fast" and "Take a rocket, from your pocket." His winter poem showed the use of repetition:

> The snowman comes white as white,
> A chill in the air,
> Winter is here.
> The snowman comes, the snowman goes.
> Winter was here and winter was there
> The snowman goes, the snow does go,
> Everything goes when winter goes.

A perfunctory poem, to say the least, but at the same time he had turned in this one:

> Beans, beans the musical fruit,
> the more you eat the more you toot
> the more you toot the better you feel
> so beans, beans, at every meal.

Here rhyme was extremely well used, as well as cadence; so much so, in fact, that I wondered whether it was original. In his second tide pool poem, John used no rhyme:

> Squishy animals in rocky shallow pools
> Purple sea urchins with spiny prickles

> Tiny hermit crabs in abandoned shells.
> Ugly and pretty, strange and weird.
> Once filled with creatures of the shore,
> Slowly disappearing from the pools.
> Collectors come and leave with animals.
> How shall we protect the tide pools?

In a poem about dreams, he wrote,

> I walking down a road
> I find this house,
> I go inside,
> Monsters charge
> Right at me.
> Weird, spooky,
> Ugly, green,
> And then I wake up.

Four days later he was back to rhyme:

DRIVING

> When you drive you look around
> Everywhere, I mean everywhere, even the ground.
> Driving is a sort of transportation.
> Sometimes on a vacation.
> Driving is sometimes good
> And sometimes sad
> Because some people drive pretty bad.

One could question here the accuracy of "sad," or the leap from "transportation" to "vacation," but I felt it better, at this point, to ignore his experimentation. A cinquain, telling of a moon "sometimes foggy/and it is sometimes very pretty/and sweet" said exactly nothing. It was just at this time that I began my individual conferences with the children and, based on what I had seen, I told John to keep working, for I could now see a struggle between rhyme and non-rhyme working within him, and I wanted him to work this out for himself. His second tide pool poem showed me that, in spite of his stubbornness about changing the first, he *had* been listening and absorbing my remarks about both preaching and rhyme at the expense of sense. I cautioned him, however, about making poetry a series of statements and using words like "sad" and "pretty" and "winter was here and winter was there," and asked him to express his own feelings more, suggesting that he try to write a poem every day. The next poem he turned in was called "My Blanket."

> My blanket is very furry and soft.
> It has tiger paws on it that remind
>   you of thorns sticking in your finger.
> It's sky blue and if I stare at
> it it makes you dizzy and like your
> in a maze and can't get out.

Much better, I concluded, for John's own perceptions were beginning to come through, and meaningless rhyme had been forgotten. Indeed, his next poem, coming back to rhyme again, showed marked improvement in the rhyme and in revealing some feeling, although we can still note the wishy-washy "It wasn't real big/And it wasn't very small":

> MY TROPHY
> Yesterday I won a trophy.
> It wasn't real big
> And it wasn't very small.
> Actually, it's about one and a half feet tall.
> It gives people feeling
> About my win,

And when I think about it,
It gives me a tingle
On my skin.

Toward the end of the class sessions John was still struggling with the use of rhyme, but what he did made far more sense, and one knew he was thinking about it more clearly:

SWEAT

When I get sweaty
It seems I'm in a hot spa
It's very wet, hot and muggy.
I cool off with lots of cold water,
All the running water dripping,
And I cool off and all the sweat
And feelings disappear
Right away in a jet.

One could quibble with the ending rhyme, of course. As a teacher I can sense in John this uncertainty about rhyme (only natural for one of his age, who needs to do a great deal of experimenting), and nowhere is it more evident than in the last two poems he wrote for the class.

A ROCKET

Four, Three, Two, One,
Boom! There they go,
Off into space,
Faster, slower,
It really don't
Go on a certain pace
Get ready to land,
And stop halfway through
The journey through Space.

THE GROUND

Hard, Soft,
It can't decide
Used, Fresh,
It's always somewhere
Plants, Paint,
It gets hurt and watered.
But the ground doesn't care
As long as it's not moved.

Here the rhyming words "space"/"pace" and "some-where"/"care" make sense in the context of the poem.

To wean children away from overuse of rhyme, or poor use at the expense of sense, is a long process, and one must show that patterns, forms, repetition can take its place.

A girl like Elaine, in the University Elementary School, also feels the need of rhyme. The first two poems she turned in (we have met the first poem before, in Chapter 4) are typically poor:

Have you ever seen a tree?
It's pretty as can be.
It's nature's way of showing love
Like pretty white doves.

They're big and tall
And sometimes small
They're nice
And they intice
That is the end of the poem I began
So don't cut down the trees of our land.

WINTER

Winter is here
Summer is gone.

> Snow covers the ground.
> Why? Because winter is here.
>
> The sun goes
> Snow is here
> Sometimes rain
> And boys drinking beer.

The couplet form is undoubtedly known to Elaine, but she uses it poorly in the first poem. In the second poem, the second stanza is almost ludicrous. We know, however, that Elaine feels a need for rhyme, and this is confirmed by the next poems she turned in, after a walk outside.

A BUSH

> Gossiping old bags,
> All wearing hats,
> The garden is their garden club
> They look like old hags.

WISH

> I wish I was an eagle
> Standing so straight and tall
> I could fly all over
> Without a fall.
>
> An eagle is so proud
> He is so vain
> He never stops to anyone
> Not even a windowpane.

> Breathe deep, the best way to kill.
> Smog is on every window sill.
> The woodland creatures are dead
> Because smog is here instead.

Discussions in class of meaningless rhyme apparently reached Elaine, for the next thing she turned in focused on the possibility of repetition as a tool:

> Have you ever had a daydream?
> I like to daydream
> I like to because they send you
> Off in different lands.
> I have them all the time.
> I dream I can fly.
> Have you ever had a day dream?

Another observation poem also established the fact that she had listened, and well, to our class discussions:

> A LEAF
> A leaf looks like a hand
> With fingers branching out
> A leaf looks like a hat
> Of sophisticated ladies
>
> A leaf looks like a glove
> A velvetine glove
> That was thrown in the garbage
> Of a glove factory.

Her tide pool poem also shows use of repetition rather than rhyme:

> The feel of sand in between your
> Toes.
> The feel of starfishes in your
> Hand.
> The feel of water around you.
> That is the tide pool.
>
> To climb on rocks
> To run in the sand

> To dream of many things
> That is the tide pool.

Some reading from Carmen Bernos de Gasztold's *Prayers from the Ark* is reflected in the "pretending" poem she turned in a week later:

> DEAR GOD, LOVE, SEA HORSE
> Dear God,
>> Why do they cramp me up in a cage?
>> Why don't they let me go?
>> My wife has left me and her eggs
> I keep.
>> Oh Lord, why do they desert me?
>> Why can't I see my friends, the other
> Sea Horses?
>> I want to see my home again,
> Why can't I?
>>> *Love,*
>>> *Sea Horse*

Although one might note at this point that Elaine has left rhyme altogether, she did have to participate in exercises using the couplet, quatrain, and limerick. Nevertheless, she is content to write without it for a time:

> The anemone is vain
> She thinks her golden tentacles
>> are beautiful
> She thinks the fishes
>> who live near her, think
>> she is attractive.
> When she is insulted, she
>> stings.
> Oh yes, the anemone is vain.

The human-like seahorse clings
    to plants.
It is pregnant now.
I wonder why there is a frown
    on his face?
I wonder if he's hurt?

The lion fish roams about the
    bottom.
He is shy.
His deadly spines stick out all
    over.
I wonder what he does when
    there is a ball?

For in the sea there is a
    vain anemone, a clinging sea
    horse and a deadly lion fish.
Of course there are others
But I like these the most.
They are unique.
Why?

Elaine's next assignment was to observe and try to express her observation with feeling. Interestingly enough, she was the only child in the class who did not write a poem.

Observations

I looked at the bush, that once had blossoms, but now they were dead like an old woman losing her hair or a popcorn ball being eaten. The bird bath is dry and the birds will have to go somewhere else. They're like men in deserts who need water—looks like a vain anemone.

One could almost conclude that Elaine is afraid to go back to rhyme. She is, instead, thinking in terms of repetition, imagery, simile, and the expression of her own feelings and questions.

Yet the next poem she gave me was put into my Poetry Drawer with a note, "PLEASE DON'T READ THIS ALOUD." It is a simple ballad and it uses both rhyme and meter with great finesse. As a matter of respect for Elaine I cannot include it here.

During the class before our last, when I had assigned the children to write about the same thing as on the first day, Elaine wrote again about a tree.

> A tree in fall
> Is nothing at all.
> Like a little old lady
> Who's lost her hair.
> Spreading leaves wherever it is
> Like a god crying.
>
> I love trees.
> They stand so tall.
> I love trees
> Especially in fall.

Her poem about winter can also be compared with the earlier one on the same subject:

> In winter it rains
> It's a god's tears you see
> For a maiden has broken
>   her heart
> In winter it rains.

It is fortunate for us teachers that there are Elaines in the world, to test our own guidelines for offering forms, patterns, rhymes, repetition, and the beginning of the making of metaphor. For every Elaine there are still the many

Donnas who will not try, and the Johns who protest. But one can say goodbye to Elaine knowing that she has begun to think in terms of poetic expression, still roughly, still with much to learn, but freed from the senseless rhyming with which she began her writing.

When the class was finished I received notes from all the children. I cite the letters from John and Elaine.

A TEACHER

I had a teacher who taught me a lot,
She was a poetry teacher named Livingston.
From Mrs. Livingston I had a lot of fun.
Limerick, Cinquain, whatever it is,
I really learned a lot of things.

by John

Dear Ms. Livingston,

I hope you come back to our class again. I'm sorry I couldn't send you a poem, but I couldn't find the right words to put in it. I want to make it short so THANK YOU!

Love,
Elaine

Considering the number of poems written to me by the children in this batch of letters, the lack of rhyme becomes notable!

It needs to be said, however, that there are some children who find it difficult to use rhyme; what they turn in as poetry is little more than a prose paragraph. This often goes hand in hand with inability to use meter in any rhythmical pattern. And, carried to its extreme, in older children it becomes nothing more than a sort of personal babbling that has nothing in common with poetry save that the child has learned to write in lines rather than in a running paragraph.

Though love be a day,
Your entire life encircles it.
A simple ray of sunlite
Brings forth a new you.
Ready and willing to give
Your time and listen to
   others.
Patiently and willingly in
Order to assist them in
coping with the problems of
everyday living.
Though love be a day,
Isn't it worth it?

Janice

Aside from the lack of any poetic imagery, and the fact that this is little more than a preachment, there is nothing in these lines (save the repetition of the first line) to make one even consider calling it a poem; and yet, how many lines of just this sort are published in the name of poetry? Although I am not a stickler for punctuation, I deplore the sort of word arrangement that tries to make of this statement a poem.

For a child like this, much could be done by a teacher who would send her to the library, to read poetry in order to discover what poetry is and is not. Further, some disciplinary measures—learning about the couplet and quatrain and what makes a sensible rhyme (or what is the value of well-thought-out repetition), and about meter and what we mean by poetic imagery (love as a day seems more like gobbledegook)—might help this girl write something approaching poetry. One wonders where this child's teacher, who proudly mimeographed this "poem" for parents to see, stands in regard to poetry.

For the younger child, who has no idea of what a poem looks like, poems can be put up on a blackboard. Oftentimes, with a class that is used to writing entirely in prose, a constant rereading of simple verse like Mother Goose will work wonders. It is well, too, to put a prose composition on the board and see how it can be broken up to make a poem; for example:

I like football because when the quarterback has the ball he throws the ball to me and I run for a touchdown.

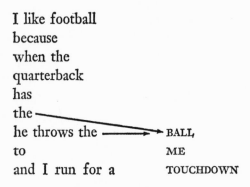

Couplets can be written as a class exercise at first, and then individually.

A bird in the tree
Looks just like me.

The sky was blue
And so are you.

A fish in water
Lost her daughter.

These examples, from a third-grade class, stress sensible rhyming words but give the children an idea of meter. In the second example it was rather easy to show the children that a different second line that was suggested, "And you are almost too," did not sound right, even to their uninitiated ears.

> There once was a cow with nine toes
> And a wart at the end of his nose,
>> You might think him ugly,
>> He's really quite snuggly
> . . . .

In this instance, at the Claremont Reading Conference, it was the teacher who had to supply the last line, "Especially in red panty hose." But the point is that the teacher was there and willing to help the children. Those who shun this responsibility are cheating the child of a joyful experience of self-expression to be found no other way.

11: Haiku: Yes or No?

SOME YEARS AGO, when Harry Behn had published his first book of haiku, *Cricket Songs*, we spoke together on the same program at the University of California, Berkeley. Harry was ecstatic over the revival of haiku that was being enjoyed and the children who were writing them. I was far less enthusiastic, for I sensed a bandwagon approach to a form that, in my opinion, is perhaps the most difficult of all to write well. Three years ago, at another poetry symposium, at Lehigh University, Harry and I talked over what had happened to haiku, and he expressed the same disenchantment I had felt originally. What had happened during those years, and, indeed, what is happening even as I write this?

Gwendolyn Brooks once told me that she began her classes in creative writing for adults by having each individual write a haiku. It gave them confidence, she told me, and the feeling that they could create a poem without rhyme. I conveyed to her, as to Harry, that it is one thing to put a set form in the hands of adults, but quite another to give it to children. Adults may well understand the rigid rules that govern haiku, but it takes an unusual child to write haiku well (just as it takes an especially talented adult).

Yet we continue to see reams of haiku written by children everywhere; haiku, that is, misnamed, for what we have ninety-nine per cent of the time is nothing but a series of words that total seventeen syllables which the teacher finds easy to teach and which by any other name would be meaningless garbage.

> I have a brown dog.
> He likes to play with his ball.
> He's a funny dog.

"Splendid," says the teacher to little Mary and proudly tacks up the "haiku" for Open House.

The second teacher, however, has read something about haiku in the flood of articles that have gone into educational magazines and journals. She has learned that a haiku always refers to something in nature.

> The lovely old trees
> Stood swaying, bending, waving
> Dropping the brown leaves.

"Beautiful," says the second teacher, and proudly mimeographs it for parents to see.

The third teacher has done a little more reading. She has learned that a haiku must have some reference to nature, must refer to one event or thing, and take place in the present.

> The forest is green
> And the tall trees stand high up
> In the blue sky.

The fourth teacher, however, has gone far beyond haiku. She has discovered the cinquain, the tanka, and even the Korean *Sijo*, and she is ready to write an article for a widely read publication. "Poetry was taboo to my 8th grade students," she writes, "but in a most devious way I've managed to let these students trick themselves into writing some of the most beautiful and tender bits of poetry [from here on referred to as "writing"] imaginable. The formula is simple: some good mood films, several different forms of writing and the creative minds of kids." She then goes on to explain that the most simple was the "Word Cinquain," with a first line that names the topic, a second line of two words that describe the topic, a third line of three words showing action and usually ending in *-ing*, a fourth line of four words forming a statement, and a fifth line of one word that summarizes. The examples of her "most tender and beautiful . . . poetry imaginable" read like this:

Buddha
Large, silent
Thinking, meditating, searching
Trying to enlarge minds
Deep

Forest:
Green, serene
Quieting, purifying, Freeing
Safety among the trees
Sanctuary

One child
Lost and alone
Crying, helpless and scared
Knowing not where to turn for love
He dies.

She goes on to tell us that "after working with five lines, the three lines of haiku were simple." The first line has five syllables, the second line seven syllables, and the third line five syllables, as you will remember. The haiku she holds up as models are these:

> Slowly shifting sand
> Carries away the footprints
> Of once trodden paths

> Gigantic sand dunes
> If this is tranquillity
> Let God make more sand

> Refractions of light
> Bring perception changes
> Man's new beginnings

> The glowing sunset
> Fading in the horizon
> Tells of darkness soon

Tanka she describes as "like haiku except there are two more lines, each with seven syllables"—in other words, a fourth and fifth line of seven syllables each, making a total of thirty-one syllables.

> False promises made
> Flashy brass bands on parade
> Long boring speeches
> Assassins on roof tops
> These the signs of politics

> I can blow a note
> It is beautifully round

Whole and pleasing to
Me. I am all new again
My heart beats with the good news.

The fact that there is a line here, and one in the haiku examples, that does not adhere to the rules does not seem to bother this teacher, who notes of all the writings that the students "were nearly as pleased with them as I was."

What is infuriating about all this is not only that the "words" bear no relationship to the forms, correctly interpreted, but that this teacher feels proud of her students' achievements and dares to tell others that the forms are *simple* and that she "in a most devious way" *tricked* the students into writing.

Tricked the students into writing what? It is more like a recitation of nouns, adjectives, verbs, preachments, statements without a voice, hollow emotions—except possibly for the last tanka, which might be a good poem if the form had not necessitated cutting off the thought in the third line. One might compare this method to any number of studies in which all that mattered was the recitation without a glimmering of understanding, or a test taken by copying an answer sheet.

This is robbing and cheating children, and such a teacher's delight in what her students have produced is false pride and dishonesty as well.

Along the way, however, we are all going to find children who have been introduced to the haiku, the cinquain, and the tanka by the sort of teacher just described. I would like a penny for every one of the children who come into my classes with reams of haiku they have written in English classes. I suspect that in their minds is the notion that writing poetry is nothing more than counting seventeen syllables and forgetting about rhyme.

My approach to this problem is twofold. In an after-school or library class I would never disparage the work of the child's English teacher, yet I deplore having the child think that he or she has mastered haiku. I usually sidestep the issue by explaining that we do not bring the writing of our English classes into a creative writing club or after-school class, and that we are going to do other things here. But the day inevitably comes when I must face up to the realities of the situation.

Without a long dissertation on the involved rules that govern the haiku, which is the beginning of a much longer Japanese form (although one can certainly explain this to high school students), I explain that the word "haiku" is made up of two Japanese words, *hai* and *ku*. *Hai* means to compose a poem; *ku* means a phrase. It is indeed, a beginning phrase (as it begins a longer poem) and is intended to be the beginning of an idea, a thought, some picture seen by the writer that will lead us on to further thoughts, thoughts of our own about what the writer of the haiku has seen or felt.

To illustrate this, I tell them the story of Basho, the great seventeenth-century Japanese poet, whose student brought him a haiku about a dragonfly. The student's haiku told of how he had plucked the wings from a dragonfly and, lo! there was a bright red pepper pod. (For the teacher who can draw, an illustration on the blackboard is helpful.) Basho explained that this was not haiku. What the student must do is to take the pepper pod, transfix wings to it, and, lo! a dragonfly!

Somehow, no matter how young, all students understand the difference. The pepper pod lies still and dead, but the dragonfly soars off to something beyond. It is a beginning.

Haiku, I go on, usually consist of seventeen syllables in

Japanese, and we try to use seventeen syllables in our own haiku. Occasionally, we may have to deviate by a syllable. We are writing in English, not Japanese.

There are rules, however, that do govern the making of haiku and that, if we are to write good haiku, we must not break. A haiku contains some reference to nature. This does not mean that we must necessarily write about a tree or a bird or a cherry blossom; we can write about a season, if we like, but we do not have to use the word "winter" or "summer" or "spring" or "fall." A cold wind may denote winter, a crocus may suggest spring, a football suggest fall, a hot sun summer. Neither do these objects need to be the subject of the haiku, but somewhere in the poem nature or a season must appear.

Haiku must also refer to a particular event, not making a broad sweeping statement about things, but describing some one thing seen or observed in our own experience, so vivid to our eyes that we make others see it. No generalizations are allowed in haiku.

Furthermore, what is happening must happen at the moment, now, rather than at some past or future time.

These are general rules, however, and oftentimes we break them if there is a good reason. But first we must learn the rules and understand them.

In haiku we must make every word count. To put in "ands" and "thes" and "buts" uses up our seventeen syllables to no avail.

Most important, I tell the students, even though it is not stated as a rule, some feeling or emotion must come through in the haiku. We are trying to re-create in the haiku a moment that will show the writer's emotion and arouse emotion in the reader, make him see something he may never have seen before. This, of course, we try to do in all poetry.

Although we know that no translation can be true to the exact Japanese, I may spend half an hour reading haiku to the children to give them an idea of what haiku can do. I am particularly fond of haiku that show humor. It is another solid point in demonstrating poetry as something that has a relationship to our everyday lives, and it helps to remove the onus of nature's Beauty, Truth, Wisdom, and cherry blossoms.

> If things were better
> for me, flies, I'd invite you
> to share my supper.
>> *Issa*
>> (*Translated by Harry Behn*)

For the teacher who wants to try haiku, I would recommend devoting an hour to the reading of a book I have found invaluable, *Wind in My Hand, the Story of Issa,* by Hanako Fukuda. I read it aloud to the class, for it shows how haiku are made up of the commonplace, and tells of the observations of Issa himself as a boy and a man, the things that were important to him and how he made them into poetry. No set of rules given to children will make them understand half as well as this book how the human emotions are part of creative writing—haiku as well as all poetry.

For the teacher who wishes to learn more of haiku for himself, Harold G. Henderson's *Haiku in English* is most concise and understandable and offers practical guidelines for judging haiku.

The writing of a collective haiku on the blackboard lends emphasis to the rules that we use in writing haiku, although I believe the technique should be a bit different here. If one child will volunteer to write a haiku aloud, it can be used as a basis for discussion of the rules, and the other children can serve as the readers. The emotions of the writer must give rise to emotions in the reader. Has the child who has written the haiku succeeded at this?

Probably the most successful haiku, written by children, that I have read occur when the voice of the child speaks to the subject of his haiku, for it is a voice felt and not a dead series of words. You will remember Albert's first poem, written at University Elementary School, which was undoubtedly meant as a haiku:

> The tall, majestic tree
> Embedded in the earth
> Beneath the clear, blue sky.

The syllable count is off, of course, but this is typical of the sort of haiku we see much too often. True, it is about nature, but nothing is happening. There is no voice here, no emotion for us to reach out and touch, simply a small picture with adjectives.

> The cherry blossom looked
> Like a pink ballerina
> Ready for dancing.

In this haiku there is a definite beginning, and the reference to nature is there. But the simile is too direct; "looked like" takes up two valuable spaces better used otherwise. Furthermore, I question whether the child who wrote this had ever really seen cherry blossoms. Haiku should be written out of one's own experience. We could easily change the tense of the verb to "looks" and adhere to the rule of something happening at the moment, but it would still not be a good haiku. Lynn, a second-grader, writes:

> Bird! Bird! Fly away!
> The big bad wolf has escaped.
> He will eat you up!

I find a certain charm in this for we feel strongly the emotion of a child.

Jason, a fourth-grader, contributed the following haiku to a Creative Writing Club session.

> Seagulls on the beach
> Almost white in the moonlight
> Going to their homes.

> Nomad, in the sun,
> Going to the oasis,
> Now, go journey forth.

> High up in the sky
> Guarding like a samurai
> Keep our fields green!

The voice addressing the big, bad wolf, the nomad, and the sun ring much truer to me than the description of the seagulls. Yet, I cannot say that in all the years I have taught I have found one haiku that I consider outstanding. Still and all, compared to the students' writing that the teacher mentioned earlier considered "beautiful," I find these efforts shining examples!

I am reminded of Babette Deutsch's statement in *The Horn Book*, some years ago, that "poetry is not a children's game." Although she intended a fuller meaning to these words, they come back to me in reference to the writing of haiku. For it has been assigned to the status of a game by

many teachers and schools today, and I deplore the misuse
to which it has been put.

I hope that those teachers who use and love the haiku
will take another look at what they are doing, recognizing
that we do an utter disservice by making the writing of this
sort of poem seem an "easy" way to create.

12: Tragedy and Comedy: Two Masks

IT IS GENERALLY conceded that perhaps one of the greatest lacks in our society, at both adult and childhood levels, is that of good humorous reading. Sociologists and psychologists may well explain the reasons for this dearth. Perhaps the problems of our society and the world itself are too numerous. But regardless of the many reasons we might be offered, the cold fact is that all of us need levity— a way of laughing at troubles and, most importantly, at ourselves.

If adults need the relief that laughter affords, children need it that much more, for we do not have to go far to see that they are worried and beset by the wars, the murders, the drug problems that stare at them on television and from the newspapers. Books of published writing by and for children attest to their concern about urban life and its problems. This is an era when we spell things out. Even audio-visual materials used in the school speak frankly to them. They are bombarded by films of the vanishing wilderness, the polluted waters, the smog problem, city gangs—the list is almost endless.

Perhaps you have noticed, as have I, that children of today do not laugh as easily as did the young people of even a decade ago. Where once a poem like Laura Richards's "Eletelephony" would produce the height of hilarity, and Lewis Carroll's "Jabberwocky" would be accepted for the delightful nonsense it is, these poems now bring less laughter, fewer smiling faces. It takes something stronger. It is interesting to me that one of the things that brings today's children the greatest delight is reacting to television commercials. They have learned, alas, that toothpastes do not always keep one from getting cavities or ensure one's popularity, that the cereal fortified with vitamins doesn't give them enough energy to go all day, and that a certain brand of peanut butter doesn't taste all that delicious. They laugh because they know that this is not reality. A strange kind of laughter.

This laughter has a way of turning into disbelief. And disbelief shatters illusions. As adults we become hardened to many unpleasant realities. But it is painful to see this in a child of the sixth or seventh grade, and sometimes much, much earlier.

Creative writing provides an outlet for some of this disillusionment. The journals and the Poetry Drawers bespeak much of it.

Two boys react, during an observation assignment, to the sound of a car honking:

Reminded me of traffic accidents, and the car trouble everybody has while driving a car. It also reminded me of air pollution which the cars' exhaust adds and how someday we might have non-gas cars. . . . .

Richard

... kind of a nuisance to the pedestrian when he hears
the rumble that could easily kill him ...

Lloyd

The world's problems are a constant source of concern
to children and turn up in many forms:

THE ZOO
The lion bristles in his cage
As you go by with peanuts
For the elephants
The elephants
The elephants

The hippos lounge in murky depths
As you go by with smelly fish
For the polar bears
The polar bears
The polar bears

The parrots scream in stinky cages
As you go by with carrots
For the zebras
The zebras
The zebras

The ghettos cry with all their dirt
As we go by with food and money
For other countries
Other countries
Other countries

Anna

MARCHING SONG
Left-right-walk in the night.
Your eyes are white, your pants are tight.

We march to the battle of bloody red,
Tomorrow we march to bury the dead.
The next day we sit in dank, wet holes
And Sabbath we stab with our bayonet poles.
Left. Left. Never right,
And never wrong
Till we see the light.
So says the song (as we get shot)
Never thinking a dangerous thought.
Backward, backward—onward we fought.
We silently march to bury the dead.
We march from the battle of bloody red.
Left. Left. Left. Left.
but Right? Right? Right? Right?

Lloyd

HIS FACE

Between the eyes—between this nose
  is what I'm after.
  The covering doesn't matter.
Why?
This face—100 years of hallowed patriotism ago,
  It moved and laughed,
  and . . . kissed.
Now they say we can see it,
  I can't even remember from the last look.
  Maybe, if I looked some more.
I can't see him. I know him . . . He's beautiful . . . no. I
  must control my emotions—I can't see them on that
  plastic face;
  I smell honor.
Don't worry! You're tired!
So am I!

So am I!
United:
You brought forth; I take; some day I'll give.
Why?
It's cold and nothing's left but a state of mind,
    and, if that's not enough, and it is not enough
Then I've got a lot of planting to do, and, Mr. Lincoln,
The black tie is optional.

                           Mark

Poems marking the assassination of John Fitzgerald Kennedy, Martin Luther King, Robert Kennedy, Malcolm X; political poems questioning the policies of the Governor, the President; a simple plea from Pam, a fifth-grader:

       I hope that at least
       The world would be at peace . . .

These concerns seem to dominate much of the writing. It is of utmost importance that we accept whatever the children are thinking about the serious nature of things, but it is also important that we try to encourage their lighter side in every way that we can.

In all of the writing we assign, in all of the variations of forms and disciplines, we need to explore and strongly encourage the many possibilities for humor.

Some children, of course, have a sense of humor or a natural wit that comes as a pleasant surprise to the teacher. At University Elementary School, Karen was at her best in light verse, nonsense, and silliness:

       Should puzzles wear muzzles,
       Or should muzzles wear puzzles?
       For when puzzles aren't solved
       They gnash their befuzzles. . . .

Her inexperience with rhyme and meter does not obscure
the chuckles behind this "pretending" poem:

> A bookworm I am,
> And one I'll always be
> As I feast on the book
> "Bury My Heart at Wounded Knee."
> The greatest dictionaries,
> Encyclopedias too,
> can be found in my stomach
> be them old or new
> "Journey to the Center of
> the Earth" as well as
> favorite "Cricket on the Hearth"
> are in my stomach
> As well as countless volumes
> Of Look and Life and UCK!
> Now I got indigestion,
> A pain in the Funk & Wagnall
> Which will hurt and bother
> me until I turn diagonal.

An assignment in the use of repetition produced this one:

> It's just one of those days;
> I fell in the gulley and after
> I put my shoes in my locker today
> Somebody stole them.
>
> It's just been one of those days;
> My best friend moved away and
> With her she took my science
> Report.

Alexandra also responded, with great humor, to the repetition assignment:

What's repetition?
This is repetition. This is repetition.
This is repetition. This is repetition.
   etc. etc.

Craig caught the spirit of our constant reference to the repetition used in Langston Hughes's "Poem."

This is a poem about nothings
Which is a sort of nothingless something
It is something of nothing
And nothing of everything
This poem ends as weirdly as it began . . .
A nothing is something of everything.

In spite of its obvious faults and confusion over rhyming patterns, there is good humor in this poem by James:

What a goof to act aloof
At a party with Bill and Marty

Bill said to me, "Hey Mr. Cool
Go jump in the pool" and then Marty
"Ya Mr. Fake, go jump in the lake!"

I did just that—I jumped in a lake
Not of water but of thought.

Which really taught
Me a lesson.

The cinquain assignment also provided a jumping-off place for Alexandra's wit:

"Look, look"
"Look look at what?"
"Look at that over there"

"Look at what over where; I can't see it."
"Too late."

John S., too, found a place for his humor in the cinquain:

> The cave
> The cave has a
> The cave has a giant
> The cave has a great ugly
> Cave man!

Karen again, working on couplets, wrote:

> I bought a pickle
> For a nickel.
>
> It crunched
> As I munched.
>
> I bought a pickle
> For a nickel
>
> I think I'll buy a bunch.

The way in which some children use humor to admonish adults is astonishing and extremely amusing. At University Elementary School there were often visitors attending the classes, and James expressed his reaction this way:

> Visitors
> How I hate Visitors
> Who look over my shoulder
> Who ask me questions
> And annoy me.

Craig, resisting my suggestion that he write something about his wishes, turned in this:

I don't have any wishes, no, not at the moment
I don't have any, oh please don't shout
Maybe tomorrow no don't start to pout
I haven't any, whosoever, whatsoever,
    howsoever. . . . . .
. . . . and that's that

> *By the Great*
> *Super Stupendous*
> *Craig*

Another time, given an assignment to write, for the second time, on buildings, Craig wrote:

Old and new
Red and blue
Any color you want
Buildings are hard to write about
Because there's nothing to write about
and besides . . . .
. . . .
. . . .
. . . . . I don't want to

The limerick, of course, is a natural for the expression of funny situations, and nonsensical names and places:

There once was a woman of Mazy
Who thought that her old man was crazy
    She sent him to bed
    And bashed in his head
And now he's as sweet as a daisy.

> *Alexandra*

There was a young man named McNoon
Who wanted to go to the moon

He went in a car
But did not get far
That foolish young man named McNoon.
                    Lisa

There was a young woman from Shell
Who argued uncommonly well
        All these words, words, words, words
        Said her spouse, are absurd
And threw her down Calanan's Well.
                    Julie

Dana's sense of humor and his smile were infectious, and one day when he had struggled for almost an hour with the first four lines of a limerick, I had to come to his rescue and suggest a fifth:

There was an old donkey of Hatin
Who thought he could speak fluent Latin
        He woke up one day
        And wanted to say
"I *semper* wake up in the *matin*."

Beyond the fifth- and sixth-grade levels the humor is apt to become more sophisticated.

There once was a girl from New York
Who tried to sip soup with a fork.
        She tried and she tried,
        But finally replied
"It's hard to sip soup with a fork."
                    Tracy

There once was a cockroach that said
"I think I shall sleep in your bed.

> It's comfy and soft,
> A luxurious loft,
> And I'll stay if I'm very well fed."
>
> *Lori*

Humor can creep into observation quite easily. Jared, in seventh grade, was asked to observe the nose of his neighbor to the right:

> Wiggly; ready to sneeze; ready to take off in outer space alone like a future capsule exploring something new.

The natural punster will find that this form of humor also can be utilized in creative writing. Edwin, who was in one of the after-school classes in Beverly Hills, would spark all of his writing with double meanings. Sent out on a walk to observe, he returned with this saying:

> "I cannot be deFEETed as I look to the ground—but walking like that for a whole block?"

His limericks focused on the same thing:

> There was a man born just a head
> So he took a whole body instead,
>   But the heart was amiss
>   And the moral is this,
> You should always quit while you're a head.

Many children will cling to nonsense and silliness to the point of absurdity, often in an effort to draw attention to themselves. Others have a better sense of when humor is wanted. The young child will use rhyming as a spur to nonsense. A boy like Lloyd, in the ninth grade, can turn the simplest assignment (why not write an *ABC*?) into delightful humor:

ORATION

A	Mexican hat is not to
Be	undermined, especially when one can
Cee	its innate qualities which
Dee	golden color rev-
Eals.	However
F	one doesn't see the beauty:
G-	whiz- let them go to
H	or heaven but
I	do not think that they should be on this earth, or
Jail.	Yes, the people of Castapec have pride, "¿Peru,
K	dices? No me gusta el sombrero."
"L	sombrero es bonito, pero no le quiero."
M-	prisoned him yes that's what I say. The art is not for his
N-	tertainment. Should we throw pearls before swine?
O	no. Let them watch their
P's	and
Q's	But then again—
R	we insinuating that "el sombrero no
S	bonito. No, el sombrero es pare
T.	"It's for
U	to enjoy—to wear.
V	want you to wear it!
W	wear it!
X	communicate not, the Mexican's straw hat:
Zer Guht!	

Concern for the world, eyes open to the problems and distresses of life—yes. We cannot shut our ears and eyes to these. But let us, as teachers, attempt to round things out a bit by keeping our eyes and ears open for those whose sense of humor shines through, no matter what the focus is in our class sessions.

And let us share poetry with children that stresses the humorous as a way of looking at life through laughter. Lewis Carroll, A. E. Housman, Edward Lear, and the many anthologies that focus on the lighter way of seeing things. Cautionary rhymes, *Slovenly Peter*, Hilaire Belloc, David McCord, books such as Maurice Sendak's *Pierre*, Sorche Nic Leodhas's *There's Always Room for One More* —these are only a beginning. Both words and pictures have a way of letting children, no matter what their age, know that laughter is important. I have read the nonsense alphabets of Edward Lear to all ages. No one is ever too old for a laugh, nor ever too young.

Kornei Chukovsky, the Russian poet and educator whose work has been recognized widely in this country, speaks of the child in *From Two to Five*. Children of this age, Chukovsky tells us, believe

> that life is meant only for joy, for limitless happiness, and this belief is one of the most important conditions for their normal psychological growth. The gigantic task of the child in mastering the spiritual heritage of the adult world is realized only when he is satisfied with the world that surrounds him. This is the source of his incentive and strength to wage the struggle for happiness which the individual carries on even during the most trying periods of his life.

Chukovsky believes that nonsense verse, or "topsy-turvys," provides a richness for the child because "every departure from the normal strengthens his conception of the normal." This "verifying" and "self-examination . . . increases the child's self-esteem as well as his confidence in intellectual abilities" because he recognizes what is wrong and what is right. Nonsense also develops (not insignificantly), he notes, a sense of humor.

> It is a precious quality which will increase the child's sense of perspective and his tolerance, as he grows up, of unpleasant situations, and it will enable him to rise above pettiness and wrangling.

If we believe, with Chukovsky, that the nonsense which the youngest child hears or makes up develops and strengthens his sense of humor and increases his perspective and his tolerance of unpleasant situations, why is it not the same for the child of six to sixteen? Given the child who is not exposed to nursery rhymes or nonsense verse outside the classroom, who may come to this point of growth long after he is two, three, four, or five, should we not, as teachers hopeful of fostering the potential within him and of helping him wage the struggle for happiness, encourage the humor, the nonsense, the laughter, that he is capable of creating?

13: Getting to the Non-Writer

IN AN AVERAGE classroom, sometimes even in a special group of children who purportedly come to enjoy creative writing, there will always be those who find self-expression extremely difficult. I remember particularly one eighth-grader a number of years ago who voluntarily enrolled in an Extended Day Class in Creative Writing. He was an excellent student and an intelligent boy, but every class assignment resulted in the most perfunctory writing imaginable. His journal read like a diary: "Got up. Ate breakfast. Walked to school. Came home. Studied. Ate dinner. Studied. Went to bed." His observation papers were notable for lack of response to almost any given object. Nonsense poems, limericks, portraits in words, ballads, epitaphs—nothing seemed to arouse his imagination or stimulate expression. I was curious as to why he had come to the class and learned that, as is sometimes the case, his mother thought it would improve his English composition. I had other thoughts in mind for his development.

But alas! An entire year produced nothing that could

even approach creative writing, and in my concern—was I a complete failure?—I discussed him with one of his English teachers. It was some relief to learn that she, too, had despaired of the boy's imagination. "One day," she told me, "I hit upon what I thought would be a wonderful solution— I brought him a flower. And do you know what he did with it? He sat down and counted the petals."

We will, as teachers, always meet with these extremes. But if children are given a wide range of chances for expression and a variety of forms, as well as instruction in using the tools, we can hope for something better in most of them.

Robin is typical of the child to whom creative writing comes hard. The first poem she turned in at the University Elementary School sessions was written, of course, after encouragement to express feeling.

> THAT PEAR BLOSSOM TREE
> It's tall and beautiful, with everything
> that is suitable to me.
> I like it very much That Pear Blossom
> tree; because it is adding something to
> natures world. And if every tree could
> be like my Pear Blossom Tree, I don't
> know what I would do Id be so
> happy.

Her two poems on winter follow in the same vein:

> Winter is a wheather which things
>   usually don't grow.
> It's cold and some times windy.
> It is sometimes gloomy and gray, but
> now spring is coming so winter will soon
> be far away.

I like winter because it sometimes snows.
And when I ask my mother she never says "NO".
I play with my friends and my friends play
    with me.
I like winter and winter likes me.

Robin's observations, a few days later, showed dull reactions to things. This made her "happy," that made her
"cold." There was a faint glimmer of hope, however, when
she saw something that "made me feel like I want to go
someplace." A few days later, when I gave each of the children a potato chip to eat for taste reaction, I was much encouraged by her response: "You can hear yourself crunch."
Two classes later, she turned in a poem:

MY DREAM

My dream was a weird one
With all sorts of funny fun.
As I was walking I saw a
man who looked very weird
And on his face he had a long
bierd.
As I started to say "hi" he all
of a sudden disappeared.
I was very startled and started
to walk away, but before I knew
it I was up again.

Robin is discovering the possibilities of rhyme to hold her
words together, although it is here used poorly. But I was
less concerned with form than in getting her to express her
feelings, which is hardly accomplished by the use of the
word "startled."
Her cinquain means almost nothing:

> If I
> could drive a car,
> I would forget how to,
> When I learned how again I'd be
> happy.

Although she has become conversant with the possibilities of form and rhyme (as in the dream poem) and shows that she is beginning to understand the difference between prose and poetry through class discussions, in my conference with Robin I urged her to abandon worries about form and rhyme for a bit and concentrate on expressing her feelings. Her tide pool effort shows the slightest shift, toward the end, from fact to feeling, although here again "interesting" and "neat" are used as ends, rather than as means to expression.

> The tidepools are a nice place
> where you can see a lot of different
> kinds of Sea Animals; like the
> sea anemones, and how it sprays
> water at you, and the hermit crab
> and how it walks around with
> its shell. It is very interesting. It
> makes me feel funny when I touch
> different kinds of skin. Like the sponge
> is soft and when you touch a
> sand dollar it has very rough. They
> really all feel very neat.

Robin's first attempt at a limerick shows how much of a struggle rhythm and metrics are for her:

> There was an old bulldog from Spice
> Who was so extremely nice

But when he tripped over
A big four leaf clover
He was mad, he fell on some ice.

Asked to write something from a journal observation, she
continues to have difficulty with rhyme and meter:

Today I saw a palm tree
   with long thorny leaves.
They looked like little green
   things, who were most likely
   to be thieves.
But when I touched one of them
   it didn't feel like that.
It felt like a doctor giving
   me a shot, who was big,
   mean and fat.

At this point a teacher feels a certain amount of disappointment, for surely this is the poorest kind of rhyme,
and the first simile is as far-fetched as can be imagined. Yet,
one has to take heart because at least Robin is beginning
to use her imagination, to tell us how she reacts to things,
and she has begun to grasp something about the form of
poetry.

Told one day in class that she might write about anything
she wished, she turned in more writing than anyone else:

SUMMER

Summer isn't always hot it's sometimes cool.
What I like about it, is you can
   travel, go places without worrying
   about having to go back to school.
You can go to the beach and
   swim which is a lot of fun. You

can take a tan out in the sun.
Boy, is summer a lot of fun.

MY WISH
I wish that this year that
the graduates would win
the faculty in this years game.
The faculty always wins and
that's the same.
Everyone knows we will win
because we are better than them
so of course we will win.

POLLUTION
Pollution is bad for you.
People don't think about themselves
So why don't we start thinking about
someone else
As they always say . . . . Give a Hoot
Don't Pollute

The flaws in grammar, in overuse of repetition, in form, and in metrics are so apparent here as to make a teacher wonder whether anything she has done is worthwhile. Yet one must remember that Robin, in comparison to some of the others, is not a child to whom writing and self-expression come easily. This is a time for patience, for praising Robin for beginning to understand how poetry differs in form from prose, for expressing her feelings about her wish and her concern for pollution. It is a time to remind her that when she rhymed "school" with "cool" and "fun" with "sun" it was a natural and good rhyme. It is time to give her special practice in metrics, and to urge her to go to the library and read more poetry. It is time to further encourage her toward self-expression, to discuss with her, again in conference, how important it is in writing poetry to see something new, something that no one else sees, and, by communicating this, make a poem.

The last week of class, Robin was given an assignment to go back outside and observe. She turned in the following:

> The trash can that I see is
> different.
> If you were to turn it up
> side down you could wear
> it as a hat.

> The bushes leaves look like a
> turkies feathers all bunched
> up into one circle
> It spreds out all over like the
> wind had blown it out into a
> wide fan.

> I see a building, it is quite tall.
> It doesn't look like it's hand
> made.
> It smells like cement and looks
> like a lego building.

> This chair looks like a hard
> throne.

Robin has undoubtedly come, through class discussion, to a discovery of simile. The bushes that look like turkey feathers, the building that looks as though it were made of Lego blocks, and the chair that looks like a throne offer

new possibilities to Robin's imagination. They are not finished poems, but they show a growth in her self-expression.
Given a longer time, the teacher could help to expand these
images, but as it is, one must point out to her that there is
more strength in her first effort, for it does not rely on
"looks like a," which is a waste of words. As it happens, the
teacher rejoices for the breakthrough and for Robin's beginning feeling for better rhythm and lack of meaningless
rhyme.

On the same day Robin also wrote this:

> One day our teacher said that
> we were going to study Sports
> O.K.?
>
> Everybody said "Yes Teacher" because
> they were all happy that day.
>
> Then teacher said, "no," I think
> we'll study Abraham's toe.
>
> Everyone said, "Oh Gee, why
> can't we study Washington's knee?"
>
> The teacher said, "Oh foam,
> I think it's time to go home."
>
> Everyone ran and said "That's
> a mation, boy are we lucky
> it's Easter vacation."

In spite of the absolute nonsense of "mation," this is a very
interesting verse, seen in the light of Robin's other work,
because for the first time we see the emergence of a sense
of humor. Robin has been struggling to become conversant
with the writing of poetry. It has not come easily to her.

Yet she has not lost a certain joy about it, and this is urgently important.

A vacation assignment to write a limerick shows how far she has come. Though far from metrically perfect, and certainly not particularly humorous, it is a vast improvement over her first limerick.

> There was a young duckling from West,
> Who everyone said was a pest,
>> Then one day he said
>> Why don't we go to bed
> And then that will give us a rest.

Robin's last two poems, given below, are far from the best in the class, but they show that something is happening—that she has absorbed the admonitions to use her eyes and ears and feelings. If we contrast them to her first poems about a tree and winter, we will feel that, even if we have not produced first-rate poetry, we may at least have helped her own self-image and powers of expression to grow.

A TREE

> This tree reminds me of a
>> chickens feet
> With long golden and green
>> feathers.
> It is planted in the dirt's
>> root
> And blows in stormy weathers.
> But when it is hot it just
>> sits there with no one, all
>> alone.
> But someone comes, they run
>> around in order not to be
>> found.

So its not alone it has someone and it is happy.

Winter is fun. I like it
Especially when it snows.
Your feet get cold, and the
snow tingles your toes.
Your face starts to freeze
and so does your nose.
And sometimes winter is hot
and I like that a lot.

There are, however, a number of children who seem unable to be helped, who will end up writing just as they began, whose lack of imagination and sensitivity becomes not only a tremendous challenge but a mark of failure, as well, to the teacher. I have known a few such children, and my own inability to inspire them has left me downcast. Sometimes I sense that the child has personal problems so grave that opening up emotions and feelings through creative writing is impossible. Oftentimes, there are reading and writing difficulties. And some children, like some adults, simply find creative writing a downright bore. The football field, the movement of a dance—almost any other area will satisfy them more fully, allow their self-expression to flourish.

We must recognize this and know that creative writing is not for everybody. But given a classroom full of children, it would seem urgent to proceed from the premise that within each individual lies a need for self-expression, and it may be met through the writing of poetry and the encouragement that we give. When Chukovsky speaks of the dangers of educators who are teaching narration, he might well be speaking of the English teacher in any city in any country:

> If he is too exacting with his constant corrections, he represses the child's free expression of his feelings and ideas and does not leave room for his emotional and mental gropings. He thus risks fading the color out of the child's speech, making it anemic and devitalized, killing in it its wonderful childishness and inflicting a permanent harm.

Oftentimes we get children to whom the harm has already been done. The child has learned to use "nice" and "pretty" and "cute" as substitutes for his own feelings. The child has been taught to repress his own reactions to things about him and respond in clichés: "The winter is cold," "The summer is hot," "Leaves fall in the autumn," "Christmas brings good cheer." We have touched on all of this in foregoing chapters, but it seems well to reiterate that we must be constantly vigilant for this sort of response, and, for the short time the children are with us, try to instill in them a love of fresh expression, help them to find that spark of "linguistic genius" (as Chukovsky puts it) with which they were born.

We can further this effort not only by our teaching of the importance of individual sensitivity but also by individual conference. Praise should be given; there is not one child writing in whose work one cannot find something to commend, as well as criticize.

In my own conference notes for the University Elementary School class, I find myself writing:

YOU HAVE A GOOD SENSE OF HUMOR. THINK MORE ABOUT YOUR FEELINGS (I KNOW YOU HAVE THEM). YOU'VE TURNED IN SOME EXCELLENT OBSERVATIONS. YOUR DRIV-

ING POEM SHOWS PROGRESS. WE WILL LEARN MORE
ABOUT FORM BUT MEANWHILE LOOK AT POEMS IN BOOKS.
NOTICE HOW WE WRITE IN LINES.

YOU'VE DONE SOME NICE WORK. IF YOU WANT TO USE
RHYME YOU NEED TO THINK MORE ABOUT HOW TO USE
IT SO IT MAKES MORE SENSE. KEEP ON WRITING EVERY
DAY. READ POETRY.

I NEED TO KNOW WHAT YOU ARE THINKING. YOU ARE
TELLING ME ONLY THINGS AND FACTS I KNOW ALREADY.
PLEASE DON'T USE RHYME FOR A WHILE BECAUSE IT GETS
IN THE WAY OF YOUR FEELINGS. I LIKED HOW YOU FELT
ABOUT TOUCHING THE BARK OF THE TREE. IT MADE ME
FEEL I WAS TOUCHING IT TOO.

I AM REALLY PLEASED WITH YOUR IMPROVEMENT. YOUR
OBSERVATIONS ARE MUCH BETTER. YOU HAVE GOOD
RHYTHM IN EVERYTHING YOU WRITE. KEEP WORKING
ON YOUR FEELINGS.

Mrs. de la Sota included in the Observation Center a
series of reminders to the children that worked very well
for them and might well be used in other classrooms, as the
points are discussed in class.

1. Poetry does not have to rhyme
2. Anything in the world can be the subject of a
   poem
3. You can't write a meaningful poem without feeling
   strongly about it
4. You don't have to worry about spelling until after
   your poem is written and you want to share it
5. Poetry is more than a series of facts or statements

6. Word pictures are the art of poetry
7. Every word counts in poetry
8. Poetry is imagination and imagery
9. You can communicate an idea or feeling by comparing two things
10. Poetry is "the best choice of words"
11. Rhyme is a tool of poetry to be used properly, not artificially
12. Punctuation is for the purpose of making a poem easier to read

Keeping a folder of each child's work is invaluable in making the individual conference a working exchange. One can point out where rhyme has ruined the sense, where rhythm has gone off, where a factual statement has been used instead of feelings, where a cliché has interfered with the possibility of fresh observation. I have always made it a point either to keep all of a child's work until the end of a semester, or to recopy it so that I can keep abreast of his growth and/or stumbling blocks. I have learned the hard way that writing children take home often ends up in the trash can or stuffed away in a drawer, and then the teacher has no firm basis on which to judge what is happening to the development of the child.

The amazing thing to me is that children are well aware of their own strengths and weaknesses in many areas and, given attention, will respond well to suggestions. This is more than half the battle of getting to the non-writer.

14: Gifted or Not?

Am I capable of recognizing poetry if I come across it? Do I possess the organ by which poetry is perceived? The majority of civilised mankind notoriously and indisputably do not; who has certified me that I am one of the minority who do? I may know what I like and admire, I may like and admire it intensely; but what makes me think that it is poetry? Is my reason for thinking so anything more than this: that poetry is generally esteemed the highest form of literature, and that my opinion of myself forbids me to believe that what I most like and admire is anything short of the highest? Yet why be unwilling to admit that perhaps you cannot perceive poetry? Why think it necessary to your self-respect that you should? How many saints and heroes have possessed this faculty?

A. E. HOUSMAN's words admonish me as I speak of the lack of quality in many poems cited throughout this book and as I now take up writing that comes nearer to being poetry. We are apt, says Housman, often to admire poetry for the wrong reasons, "not really admiring the poetry of the passage, but something else in it." Pleasure, he tells us, can often be derived from other ingredients.

This *pleasure,* for me, comes not because anything I have taught to young people results in the perfect polished poem. I take pleasure in the idea a poem may express, or in its original turn; delight in an image as seen through young eyes; joy in a few lines that may represent growth. Many things about the poems are delightful, others may still need much work.

But I must know my own standards for these things and uphold them, offering praise when it is deserved, but criticism when it may be helpful. Which leads me, in a certain sense, to the conclusion that much of the work done by children in the classroom today is beneath the standards we should set for it. What we do see, in the published books of children's writing edited by adults and in a number of magazines, usually represents the best. What disturbs me is the false praise given to children's writing in school publications, bound sheaves of writing displayed at book fairs, mimeographed pamphlets, and "examples," sometimes elaborately printed, of outstanding writing, thus:

BLUE SKY

A man once told me
Many years ago
To find a blue sky
And he would reward me
With much gold.

The task was very easy
For all I had to do
Was to shout aloud
"Why, look above you!"

A man just told me
Yesterday or so
To find a blue sky
And he would reward me
With much gold.

I looked near and far
But no luck came to me
The skies were gray
As far as I could see

And I went home that night
Empty handedly.
Roxann

The places where pollution
are never seen
    May be few and in
    between,
But I'm sure somewhere
peoples hopes are high
    so that maybe
    someday they'll stop
    and try
To find a link in the
very long chain
    That could help to
    stimulate someone's
    brain,
So that they too will get
involved
    In helping this
    world to evolve.
Shari

We do not help children to write well, to grow, to reach, by publishing this work as "excellent examples" of poetry. Indeed, we do them a great disservice. Both are typical of what Cleanth Brooks and Robert Penn Warren, in their textbook *Understanding Poetry*, refer to as "message hunting" in poetry. The ecological concerns of these children undoubtedly appealed to the teacher, but given the strong feelings and expression inherent in the work, how much more the teacher might have done to help these children learn something about the making of a real poem.

To recognize the poem that is truly a contribution, I think we ourselves must understand the difference between high-flown thoughts that say nothing and honest expression of a child's feeling. Oftentimes this is difficult to do. We have spoken before of the danger of simile and metaphor obscuring any measure of feeling, of long strings of adjectives masking a human reaction, of a syllable count substituting for the real meat of emotion in the haiku or cinquain, of rhyming couplets or quatrains masquerading as real poetry.

The child who does an outstanding piece of writing is not above succumbing to any of these faults, but there shines through the stumblings and inadequacies an individual voice that compels us to listen: he has mastered the rules as well as his age allows.

> The faith in an accidental arrangement that can be asserted as a work of art has helped many writers to justify to themselves a kind of poetry in which no particular human voice is to be heard. To me, poetry has to offer such a voice and to control its cadences, its inflections, and its emphasis in some indestructible order.

X. J. Kennedy is speaking. We must admit that we cannot expect in our children's writing the control of cadence, the inflection, and the emphasis we look for in the works of a polished poet, but we must insist on the individual voice and some measure of understanding of the rules that govern the making of a poem.

As a high school student I studied counterpoint with Darius Milhaud at a summer session at Mills College. One morning I took an exercise I had completed and placed it on the piano for M. Milhaud to play. He looked at the music, put his hands on the keyboard, and played my exercise through. Then his eyes left the music and he turned and looked me straight in the eye. "Miss Cohn," he said, and the memory of that voice has stayed with me forever, "we must always learn the rules before we can break them."

I have carried this as one of the credos of my life, and I repeat the story to students today. No doubt I repeat it more often to the student in whom I find much promise as a potential writer and to those who have exhibited a natural talent for writing poetry. My standards, therefore, vary. I am not as likely to insist on perfection in the Robins I meet, for I am struggling to bring out that inner voice that needs to be heard, but once I have heard the inner voice I become a disciplinarian. I want the young people to live up to their potential.

Lloyd started as a member of our Extended Day Class in Creative Writing in the seventh grade. One day he turned in a poem about the desert.

> I look out on an endless plain of white sand;
> It glitters in the lifeless sun.
> Here I stand . . .

> All is white, and never a green impurity,
> Save a blue-white sun; and a sky of death.
> Here I lie . . .
>
> I'm forever trapped beneath the piling sand.
> Under a white plain;
> A desolate land . . .

From almost anyone else in the class, I would find this acceptable. From Lloyd, I felt it less than he was capable of producing. This was neither the full measure of his voice nor worthy of the form he could produce. I felt empathy for his view of the desert (it happens to be one I share), but I could not give the poem praise. His observations, his journal entries, his natural ability with meter and rhyme, as evidenced in class exercises and in an original composition he had played for us on the piano, made it obvious that the desert poem was far less than Lloyd, at age eleven, could do. He had also turned in a piece of writing based on a class assignment to "walk" and then "ride" down a few blocks:

"AFTER RIDING DOWN THE SUNSET STRIP"
> On a Saturday evening a strange thing happened,
> Or was it strange at all for the geographical location?
> Out of nowhere came limping, loping hairy beasts set
>   upon the world by their breeders who specialize
>   in raising their sort.
> Walking among the herd was what seemed to be the
>   leader of the strange beasts,
> Decorated with the medals and honors of the
>   civilization.
> His trinkets ranged from the "Legalize Abortion"
>   medal to "All the way with the Life-Saving-
>   Drug."

When he received such a high place in his natural
     environment and was idolized by the society of
     his sect which was of the typical Sunsetoid race,
His appearance was rather gruesome for he had not
     yet been public-broken by his breeders.
His head somewhat resembled a pin cushion completely
     full of very long pins.
He was dressed in a one-piece terry-cloth garment
     that consisted of his highly esteemed medals and
     the colors: blue, orange, pink, yellow and black.
     Truly, he was the idol of his fellow semi-humans.
He walked with a drunken limp and finally disappeared
     in the midst of the mob headed for the throng
     which was already proceeding. To celebrate
     what? . . . .

I knew what Lloyd was capable of doing and I saw in his
work that mark of originality that comes far too seldom. I
knew that his voice was unique. What could I do to further
his ability?

I did not give him more than a sprinkling of exercises in
the couplet, the quatrain, or metrical patterns. I did introduce him to the ballade, the ballad, the sonnet, the triolet, but I also allowed him to struggle toward finding his
own forms.

In the eighth grade, at twelve years old, he was writing:

ALLEY

Dead black moves in the alley
Cat bright white eyes
hunching his seemingly
powerful back.

Let out a chilling cry
To freeze grey dead

resounding through foggy air
without a white moon.

Silver garbage cans against,
against rusty orange walls
set in hard cold brick
and rough cement.
Cement almost as hard and
cruel as the cat's scream.

LONELINESS

A sphere dropped down, down
Making no noise at all.
Going through consistent darkness,
Value.
Into black it fell and into
                        black it fell,
Never a sound.

Lloyd was listening to our discussions about the use of repetition, about form; he was experimenting and becoming acquainted with the possibilities of rhyme:

COLORS

Red
    Blue
        Green
            Orange
                Yellow
                    Purple—

These are happy colors,
                Black!

OneTwoThreeFour
Infinity comes to knock at my door,

FiveSixSevenEight,
It's hard to unravel a miniscule fate,
Nine, Ten—
Who will put a color to the number,
A color to the years,
A color to Life?

Deep flowing brown
Amidst an olive-green-year—
With crimson skies,
And turquoise sighs—
Silver-lining trees,
On a fleecy-white shirt—
Do the colors hurt?

A beige mountain—
Down-Black, Down-blue,
Down-Black, down-red,
Down-Black, down-purple,
   Down-Black!

And hand in hand with these experiments in rhyme and repetition goes the inner voice:

TO ALGEBRA
I'm trying to analyze this flower
By using the addition property of
  equality,
By computating the bisymmetry,
Or maybe the multiplication
  Property of Order,
By adding the yellow on the border:
  $A + B = C$ if and only if there is a number q
  such that flowers can be thought of
  either in Algebraic or Numerical terms.

The stem, I find, is 4.5253 inches
  Long.
And yet the check says I am wrong,
This flower—it does not belong
In this great and modern world.

It bends too much for my liking,
Better work out what's the matter,
Oh no— my problem almost done
Unnumerical rain begins to patter—
Computate the difference.
All in vain—
This is the breaking of my brain!

Lloyd is speaking of the struggles of the twelve-year-old, as well as of the conflict of men, regardless of age, between reason and emotion, between art and technology, between aesthetics and practicalities. His work is growing stronger; there is more of the "making of a poem" here. He seems to know instinctively when to use rhyme and when to abandon it. But when he speaks of philosophical matters, his originality never suffers—his voice remains there for all to hear. The pattern of his "Oration" (Chapter 12) also attests to this. The poems he turned in at this point fluctuated between rhyme and non-rhyme. A song, with words and music, about "Cafeteria Hamburgers" (where you "Mix a cup o' horsemeat with a pound o' oatmeal/Some eggshell and vinegar too"), a clever piece of writing on "Useful" and "Useless" presents (wherein all the useful presents became worn out and therefore ended up useless), an experimental work called "Electrucation," in which he avoids rhyme and pattern altogether, are a balance to his more formal ballades. He is feeling his way in a variety of expressions:

MR. NIXON BEWARE

Don't go left and don't go right,
Don't go straight for fear of fright,
For Mr. Nixon I've this note,
Though I'm not old enough to vote,
Mr. Nixon, say no evil—
It may cause a great upheaval.
Mr. Nixon, think no thoughts—
Or you may hear some rifle shots.
Mr. Nixon, Listen not—
For that's what you to listen ought.
Listen what I have to say,
And this besides! Sincerely pray
That you will live for four long years
Without your mouth, without your ears
And after with your senses five,
Mr. Nixon's out alive.

In the ninth grade, Lloyd was experimenting at all levels. He turned in drawings and occasional compositions for the piano. He felt at home with rhyme oftentimes and at other times used repetition. He was also playing with ideas and cadences, with the power of words:

A TRIBUTE

I don't wanna be a monk . . .
D'ya wanna, Yamata?
No . . . I don't want to play with a Hitler! . . .
Poor Uncle Tom living in a world of fantasy:
This is terrible ladies and gentlemen, this is terrible,
I'm sorry . . . I can't talk!
Kinney Car, Kinney Car.
The metabolic constituents of the seismographic
diagram are basically composed of

Jeemee, jeemee, jeemee, jeemee—
Whoa bahbee! The big guy, the little guy, the
medium guy—the Intermediate guy
Help me, No Prease
Brigita Lieluasis   Tamara Masiov

      Z A C S   Z A C S
ba!   ba!
Whatever happened to your right ear, Vincent?
Now I want to go home
More light! More light!
Is it the fourth?
So this is death . . . Well,
Is it enough?
    "IT IS ENOUGH"—
    (last words of Immanuel Kant)

One can reecognize in all of Lloyd's work a remarkable
student, one we find all too seldom in our classes, but of the
sort that make teaching a learning process for us as teachers.
We call these children gifted, and oftentimes we quake as
we recognize that we are dealing with a talent that must be
nurtured, praised at times but also inspired to do better.
The balance is delicate. We must encourage the experimentation, the new forms, and yet we must also put reins
on the moments of wild abandon if we hope to teach something of the necessity of containment. We must remember
that we give these children the rules as a background and as
discipline, but also that we must allow them the privilege
of breaking out to create new forms when the force of
what they need to say makes it necessary.

The Lloyds are few and far between, however, and we
are more likely to find, within our classes, those who show
more modest promise. They do not always turn in the

greatest number of contributions, for they are almost afraid of submitting anything that does not measure up to their self-imposed high standards of performance. For two years, every Friday afternoon, Susan sat in the Creative Writing Club at the Beverly Hills Public Library. In those two years she turned in no more than fifty lines. Yet one knew that someday she would break out into wild creativity. One tries a multitude of approaches for such a child: the introduction of many forms, the reading of literature and poetry, observation sheets, suggestions of books to read on her own, even picture books. Susan was not bored in class; she came of her own volition. Occasionally she would contribute a couplet or simply a thought:

> The fool on the hill looks down for some answers,
> But the wise man, so old and grey, looks up.

Susan's parody of Austin Dobson's "The Kiss" (Chapter 12) was the longest thing she ever completed. She would agonize over a couplet. The finest thing she ever wrote, she lost. But here again, the teacher knows that somewhere, perhaps hidden in a drawer at home, are the beginnings of future creativity.

Occasionally, a child will come as a complete surprise. Julie, at University Elementary School, dutifully turned in her poems for every class. Her winter poem showed a much better command of rhyme and metrics than most, but there was no strong voice commanding attention:

> It's dark and it's gray,
> It's sad and it's gay.
> It's winter.
>
> It's freezing outside,
> It's raining besides
> It's winter.

It comes and it goes,
It freezes your toes,
It's winter.

"The Path," turned in ten days later, departs from rhyme; there is more of a voice, but it is not a particularly interesting effort:

I saw a path, near a stream,
I wondered,
Where? I asked,
I followed.

The flowers bowed to me,
I was king.
The path led beneath the stream,
Yet I was not surprised, and I
followed.

It went on and on.
Not a tunnel, just a path.
Later, a widening space,
A room completely in marble.
I explored,
But suddenly I awoke,
All was just a dream.

Julie's "pretending poem" uses repetition rather than rhyme for containment:

ME, A PLUM TREE

It's winter now,
I'm lonely and bare
Waiting. Waiting for spring, so I may blossom
Then summer will come.
I'll drop my blossoms and bear my fruit,
My fruit of plums.

The fruit is gone and now 'tis autumn
Slowly my leaves I drop, and again,
Again it is winter.

The interesting thing about this poem, to the teacher, is that in the seventh line we have the appearance of the word " 'tis," which makes us suspect that Julie has a closer bond with poetry than we had imagined. One often finds children who are just beginning to write using a diction that they *think* means poetry—words such as "thou," "thine," "wouldst," " 'twas," " 'twere"—but at this point in the class sessions it is evident that Julie knows better.

Her limerick shows a good knowledge of meter, which confirms what we saw in her second poem about winter, and the sense is sure:

There was a young man named Tabue
Whose foot wouldn't fit in his shoe
He decided one day
To chop it away
And off came the foot of Tabue.

Another of her poems, "He Left," uses as its form three questions and tells about someone important to Julie who has left. Another poem likens an old man to a gnarled oak. She has also turned in a prayer to God praising the lovely things of nature. Her poem on spring, which serves as a contrast to her first poem, shows that she has learned something about repetition:

Soft breezes blow,
And trees sway gently
Blue skys, airy, white clouds
And always the sound of birds
trilling gayly,
All this—a part of Spring.

> Grasses green
> Flowers parading in gay colors
> And always the bright, comforting
>   sunlight
> All this, a part of Spring.

Julie's contributions are those of a child who might not strike us as being particularly gifted; yet she is more competent and in better command of the elements of poetry than most. But the voice is not very strong; it dwells on nature description for the most part.

We know that she was the child whose next contribution was the poem about the tide pool suburbs (Chapter 9). Consider, then, my own shock when she turned in a second tide pool poem.

A POET'S PARANOIA
ROBERT FROST AT THE TIDEPOOLS

> Two clams diverged in the yellow sand
> And sorry I could not grab both
> Having ready only one hand
> I reached down quick as a flash,
> Under sand and tidepool trash.
>
> Missed! took the other; he wasn't as hasty
> But still he made my chowder quite tasty.
> I left the first for another day.
> But knowing how clams can burrow away
> I supposed it would just go on its way.
>
> I shall be telling this with a sigh
> Somewhere ages and ages hence,
> Two clams diverged on the sand, and I
> Ate the slower one. But, I deny
> That it has made all the difference.

A note, on the margin of the poem, asked me to realize that "this is not very good."

What does a teacher do in this instance? Look at Julie with new eyes? Has she been not only reading Robert Frost, but understanding what he is doing in his poetry? what he is saying? Julie is in the sixth grade. She cannot be more than twelve years old. One offers such a child the widest possible range of form. Interestingly enough, although I prepared special material for her to use, she did not try the triolet, the villanelle, or the ballade. She just went on turning in the same sorts of poems shown above.

But she is gifted, and it will be fascinating to see what she does with this gift as she grows older.

"Am I capable of recognizing poetry if I come across it? Do I possess the organ by which poetry is perceived?"

15: *What the Children Find for Themselves*

T HE AUDIO-VISUAL and other teaching aids in every field that are offered to teachers are indeed staggering. Before me at this moment is yet another advertisement for a "poetry learning unit," consisting of "thought activity cards," "exploration activity cards," "focus activity cards," poetry booklets containing prose and poetry that "reflect the sensory experiences," tape cassettes that bring wind sounds and sounds of horses galloping into the classroom, scent cards with which a child can smell—indeed, the whole range of aids is here in a neat little package, including a multi-volume set of selected poetry. Before me also are record offers: recorded poetry that reminds me of what was popular when I was a child—read, to be sure, by the "greatest" voices.

Frankly, I find these aids an insult to the child and to the teacher as well. They presuppose that within the child's head there is no imagination, no remembrance of what thunder sounds like or how lilacs smell, no ability to look at one's neighbor's nose and describe it, no recall of what it is like to wake up on Christmas morning and open one's presents. They presuppose, too, that the teacher is unable to use her own imagination—to send the children out to walk and look at the ground, to discover bugs, leaves, rubbish, how it is to listen to birds singing or trucks rumbling or to smell dinner cooking or to touch a small kitten or the floor beneath one's feet. The packaged plan does exactly what "the books every child needs to get into college" do; it suggests that we are all sheep, that we respond to the same stimuli—or that, as teachers, we must rely on someone else's imagination, someone else's voice.

Commercialism will always ensure us these packaged programs—a so-called boon to the teacher who wishes to embark upon creative writing. The fact is that within our classroom, given four children or thirty-four, we have a complete "poetry learning unit" far more germane to our studies.

Given a teacher who is willing to wait patiently and allow the children their stumblings and fallings, the children themselves will make war on the overworked adjective, the timeworn cliché, the meaningless rhyme, the tired metaphor and simile. They will do this by opening their eyes and ears and becoming sensitive to what is in their environment and can never be duplicated by a set of cards and cassettes and records. They will do it by learning the joy of writing in a journal.

Children learn so much from their peers in a creative writing situation that it is a source of constant surprise. I have always been amazed in any group that, after only a few classes, my role as a teacher fades into the background. Given the ground rules about creative writing—that we see something new, or say something new about something old, that we try to listen to what we have written as well as to the writing of others, that we find something to praise and/or something that could be made better, the children are able to find for themselves where a piece of writing falls apart.

Jared, who for a year had made an effort to free himself from hackneyed rhyme, beamed as he read his cat poem one day in an Extended Day Class. He had discovered an adaptation of the cinquain that suited what he wished to say about a cat:

> He purrs.
> I see him.
> He dashes behind a tree.
> He leaves like a bolt of lightning.
> He's gone.

Steve was quick to raise his hand. "That's a cliché—like a bolt of lightning." Jared sighed and sat scratching his head. He would have to think of another way in which a cat moves.

Mark read his poem about another cat:

> Individual feet jump
> like a pad of dough
> Poke out 2 eyes
> and it will smother
> you, make sick
> noises, fall
> into your corner and
> break atmosphere
> or climb into mind
> and scratch
> I want to pull off
> and throw at ground

> but   dead
> come alive in mind
> and stings.

Steve sighed this time. He had just come into the class and was three years behind Mark in age and grade. He looked at Mark quizzically. "I don't know," he said, "your poems always sound good and they've got good words in them, but I don't understand them."

"Perhaps," I suggested to Mark, after class, for I remembered the days when his rhyming was forced, "this new style you are finding for yourself doesn't communicate—doesn't make sense to others. If you have something to say you must find a way to make it understood by others. You must learn to communicate more directly."

Anna read her cat poem:

> Shimmering, reflected in the lake
> Selene, goddess of the moon's namesake
> Fluid her movement, so unreal
> Craving, lacking a good meal. . . .

The poem finished, hands went up. "If Selene is a goddess, why does she need a 'good meal'?" they asked. "A goddess would not need food like a human cat would." Anna changed the line to "Before her, all beings kneel," and the class was happier.

Lori offered her cat poem:

> The fur ruffed on the cat's neck.
>   The eyes gleamed on the cat's face.
> The growl rolled on the cat's tongue.
>   The claws clicked on the cat's paws.
> The tail twitched on the cat's end.

The class could not decide whether or not this was a poem, but they liked the last two lines, where the "claws clicked" and the "tail twitched." Obviously, it was a perfect chance for the teacher to explain about alliteration.

Jon's turn came next:

> There's that cat
> He's so fat.
> Ate my hat.
> Stained our mat.
> There's that cat.
> He's so fat.

"Might there be too much rhyme in that?" Isabel wanted to know. We discussed the verse, deciding that it was really a sort of light verse and that the humor came through fortified by the constant rhyme. We also decided that this was real economy of words—the terseness added to the punch, as did the constant, singsong metrical pattern. Was it dactylic? Was it a series of anapests? Where did Jon want the emphasis to fall?

Then Steve read his poem:

> The cat stares, very intent,
> I have disturbed her;
> She is no longer content.
>
> Curious me, I walk toward
> Her only domain.
> Tense now, she leaves her small board
>
> And now, with silent motion
> She jumps to her kits
> And shows all her devotion.

Steve almost interrupts his own reading to tell the others, "I don't like it. I don't like the last line. It's awful. Devotion isn't right."

We talked about other possibilities. We went down the

list of rhyming words—"notion," "ocean," "commotion," "potion," "lotion." None of these would do. Steve had tried everything. Perhaps then, we agreed, he might have to change the last stanza. But we did like the tercet pattern, which hadn't been used in class before.

Inherent in all of this exchange is the notion that not only are the children growing in their writing ability by a discussion of what communicates their feelings and observations to others, but they are learning to listen as well. They have, of course, been listening to me read and recite; they have heard, on selected recordings, some poets reading their own poetry and then have tried reading it themselves. In listening to each other's work, however, they are progressing in a different way. The stumblings of one child become the concern of another, and many of the questions raised lead us to possible new solutions, new methods, and oftentimes new areas of discovery.

If Jared finds that the cliché he has used fails to strike the others, that it does not show the cat in fresh perspective, he must search out new words. He may chance upon a simile but it will have to be a strong one, for he will know that to liken the cat to lightning does not satisfy the scrutiny of his peers. In creative writing, there is no correct answer, of course; no one will mark his poem *A* or *B* or *C*, but he will know, from the class's response, how he has done.

Mark will have to learn that, having left couplets, quatrains, and other traditional forms, he may have to come back to them in some measure, in order to express himself so that others will listen. He will learn that disconnected pieces of his imagination and thoughts do not make a poem. In the process he may have to be helped by the teacher, who will attempt to speak of universal symbols, as used by T. S.

Eliot and other poets, versus the personal symbolism of some contemporary poets, which remains unintelligible, and therefore totally uncommunicative, to the reader.

Anna will have to learn that she must think carefully about rhyme and what sense it makes in terms of the subject of her poem. Lori must learn that neither techniques such as alliteration nor mere description is enough for the making of a real poem. Jon will soon have to search beyond "cat" and "fat" and "mat" and "hat," and Steve will have to learn about finding the right word and about the possible need for rewriting a poem.

And each, in open discussion, will therefore learn that poetry is not easy, but is a careful putting together of many elements to communicate feelings and experiences.

Children are also able to keep each other from becoming copycats (and also help the teacher get through some rather sticky moments). There is a tendency toward imitation among many children, when they try to write, whether of well-known poems or of the work of other children. But they are the first to catch this and spare the teacher's accusation.

A word of warning, however. When children are young they are likely to have heard a poem that, somehow, they come to feel is their own. It buries itself deep in the unconscious. As lately as ten years ago I found myself writing a poem about the circus. I began the poem, "This is the day the circus comes." It was probably two years later (the poem didn't work out and had to be discarded) that I was looking for some material for a class and found, in Rachel Field's *Taxis and Toadstools*, a poem called "Parade," beginning, "This is the day the circus comes." This can happen to a child far more easily. A third-grader turned in this poem:

Brown and furry
Caterpillar in a hurry
Take your walk
Up the long bright tree
or take your walk
To the shady leaf
or stalk.
Spin and die
To live again a butterfly.

The class expressed great approval of the poem. The teacher, at this point, can do one of two things. He can call the child up after class and explain that this is not her poem but one written, just a little differently, by Christina Rossetti. It is a lovely poem, and the child has shown great good taste in liking it so much that she has made it her own.

Or, he can pretend to remember a poem that goes

Brown and furry
Caterpillar in a hurry,
Take your walk
To the shady leaf, or stalk,
    Or what not,
Which may be of the chosen spot.
    No toad spy you.
Hovering bird of prey pass by you;
Spin and die
To live again a butterfly.

and congratulate the child, in front of the class, on remembering such a beautiful poem so well.

The child who continues to copy beyond a one-time performance must be given further help. Another third-grader, in the same class, began every poem in almost the same way, undoubtedly struggling to re-create the nursery rhyme "I Saw a Ship A-Sailing":

> I saw a boat a sailing.
> sailing down the strem
> and guess who I saw
> in it. I saw my friend

> I saw a pirate ship
> sailing on the sea. I climbed
> on the ship. I saw no one
> but (sept) me

It was best, I felt, under these circumstances, to give her a copy of the original rhyme and guide her in other writing efforts.

Children copying each other are always immediately recognized by a class. At University Elementary School, Jamie turned in a poem, which was read to the class, about hermit crabs who "look like popcorn popping." Several classes later, Fred wrote about green leaves that blow with the wind and "sound like popcorn popping." The same day Joyce said in her poem that water spiders "remind me of jumping popcorn." At the end of the class sessions Elaine noted in her observations that the bush that once had blossoms looked like an old woman losing her hair "or a popcorn ball being eaten." The poor popcorn had been played to death, and the children knew it!

The reading of poetry can always be a great help in cases of this sort: poems by different poets who see the same things in a different way. I have used animals successfully in this context; for example, Pablo Neruda's "Bestiary."

> If I could speak with birds,
> with oysters and with little lizards,

with the foxes of the Dark Forest,
with the exemplary penguins;
if the sheep,
the languid woolly lap dogs,
the cart horses would understand me;
if I could discuss things with cats,
if hens would listen to me! . . .

I want to speak with many things
and I will not leave this planet
without knowing what I came to seek,
without investigating this matter,
and people do not suffice for me,
I have to go much further
and I have to go much closer.

Therefore, gentlemen, I am going
to converse with a horse.
May the poetess excuse me,
and the professor forgive me.
My whole week is taken up,
I have to listen to a confusion of talk.

What was the name of that cat?

And Whitman:
  I think I could turn and live with animals, they are so
    placid and self contain'd,
  I stand and look at them long and long.

  They do not sweat and whine about their condition.
  They do not lie awake in the dark and weep for their
    sins,
  They do not make me sick discussing their duty to
    God,

Not one is dissatisfied, not one is demented with the
mania of owning things
Not one kneels to another, nor to his kind that lived
thousands of years ago,
Not one is respectable or unhappy over the whole
earth.
So they show their relations to me and I accept them,
They bring me tokens of myself, they evince them
plainly in their possession.

Oftentimes, depending upon the situation, I may bring a
recording of Simon and Garfunkel's "At the Zoo," or one
or two of a dozen other poems to share. The tone of the
poet, or the songster, his attitude toward animals, his seri-
ousness or flippancy, are reflected in these and many other
types of writing. And the children will, if encouraged, find
other poems and other attitudes to share.

The voices of poetry can also be discussed through such
reading and listening, as well as the varying methods by
which we make a poem. Telling the children to express
their feelings usually results, with young children, in a
poem beginning "I saw" or "I thought." Later, one can
point out that the "I" of the poem is implied, and oftentimes an objective view of what is happening is preferable.
Sometimes the poet pretends to be someone or something
else. Poems, like ballads, tell stories. Sometimes the poet
addresses his subject through conversation. At times, the
poet speaks directly to his reader.

Thus guided, the children become their own "poetry
learning unit," find their own books of poetry at the library
or at home, smell their own smells (cabbage in one house,
hot chocolate in another). They will discover the crumbs

on their own kitchen floor, the fragrant iris in their own garden, the sound of a gentle wind or a sonic boom. Thereby, they learn of their own unique selves, willing and able and yearning to grow.

"I DON'T KNOW WHAT TO WRITE ABOUT!"
Fortunately, I haven't heard this too often in the various classes I have taught, but there are children whose training demands a constant academic assignment to write. One can prove to any given group of children that the raw material for creative writing has been given to every human being.

"Close your eyes," I will say to any group from kindergarten up, "and I will tell you a story." A few skeptical children will peek at me through squinted lids, but most will listen quietly.

"Once there was a cat. He was walking in the yard one day when he decided to climb a tree. He went up the trunk, when what should fly down to the tree but a bird! The bird decided he didn't want the cat in the tree and started to swoop down upon him, pecking him and chasing him down the trunk. So the cat had to run away from the bird."

"Now open your eyes and tell me what color the cat was."

"Black," one child says. "Ginger," says another. "Yellow

and white," insists a third. "Gray," a few say. "Striped," another tells me. One child waits to be recognized. "PUR-PLE!" he shouts. A few laugh and then some other colors are mentioned—"Green and white stripes."

"And what kind of a bird is it?" I ask.

"A crow." "A robin." "A magpie." "A blue jay." "A sparrow." "A BIG BIRD WITH RED AND PURPLE DOTS AND WINGS TEN FEET LONG!" "A ONE-HUNDRED-POUND CANARY!"

"And what sort of a tree?"

"A maple." "An elm." "Poplar." "Sycamore." "A BONG TREE!"

"And the time of year?"

"Spring." "Summer." "Fall." "Winter."

It is through these various responses that even the youngest child is able to grasp quickly the idea that creative writing is made possible by the imagination, by use of the senses, for what one sees, the others may not.

But there are always the die-hards who mumble that a story is all very well, if I want to tell one, but nothing ever happens in their lives to merit writing about. For these children I carry a copy of Ellen Raskin's *Nothing Ever Happens on My Block*, a picture book that even high school students realize applies to their own situation. They quickly get the point—that if one would only turn around, he might see or hear or notice something intriguing in his environment.

Oftentimes, a reading of Robert Frost's "The Pasture" will serve as a spur to creativity.

> I'm going out to clean the pasture spring;
> I'll only stop to rake the leaves away
> (And wait to watch the water clear, I may):
> I sha'n't be gone long.—You come too.

I'm going out to fetch the little calf
That's standing by the mother. It's so young
It totters when she licks it with her tongue.
I sha'n't be gone long.—You come too.

Although I am not given to analyzing poetry, with younger children, I like to point out, through this poem, that while there are chores we all have to do, things that are expected of us in life, we must, in the midst of these tasks, take the time to look at the things that give us pleasure, and speak of them. Here, too, is experience, with its facts, used as a basis for a poem, and also the strong voice that urges the reader to "come too." Robert Frost is inviting all of us to look about us. This is a new way of looking at poetry for most young people, and what first seemed a mere "story poem" about a boy doing his chores becomes much more on many levels for children reading poetry, as well as writing it.

Observation sheets, therefore, offer unlimited possibilities for writing, whether the children start with thoughts about their own chores or look down at the ants crawling beneath their feet; whether they smell cabbage or a rose; whether they hear the sound of a hammer or of a leaky faucet; whether they taste a burned piece of toast or a candy bar; whether they stroke a kitten or touch a cactus. There is the journal, too, for recording even part of a sentence or a thought, to be worked on when there is time for more leisurely writing.

All this is raw material to be exploited.

But there are days when one's own sensibilities may seem dull, or the group is unable to find anything to respond to. In class, therefore, I might ask each child to look at his neighbor's nose, ears, or hair, and write something about them. This is an assignment that produces an inordinate amount of giggling.

We have mentioned before the value of sending the children outside to observe what is on the playground or across the street from the school. One day at the Fairburn Avenue School in Los Angeles the children came back with a raft of observations:

Lines . . . going somewhere/joining together/follow it/wanting to know where they lead to

Scott

Playground rings . . . make me feel still. Make me think like I'm in my own world, all by myself.

Cathy

The mailbox . . it looks like a hitchhiker or an old man standing at the corner watching cars go by. It makes me feel sort of lonely, very seldom being noticed.

Josh

Tree . . skinny monster with lots of hairy arms. Big black wart on his back.

House . . . a big castle with a moat around it, large blue windows—alligators—draw bridge down in front.

Nancy

What a wealth of material is here for the making of poems! I happen, also, to be a great believer in the power of a walk as homework. I will ask the children to walk a few blocks one week; the next week to walk the same blocks again watching only their feet; the next week to ride on a bicycle; the next to look from the window of a car or a bus. They become intrigued with the different viewpoints, the various sensory responses. One type of travel may assault their noses; another their ears, another their entire bodies:

> Thought of the Day: Why does Mrs. Livingston make me walk in the freezing weather outside?
>
> *Jared*

> A twig—the twig was light and crunkey. When I stepped on it—wow! It crushed.
>
> *Steve*

Lori returned with these observations:

I Saw	*I Thought*
dried up, brown leaf	. . . times when I was little and used to play in the leaves near my home in Connecticut. I also thought how sad it was that in California one misses the most glorious season of the year, autumn. I thought this was the only sign of autumn in California —a dried-up brown leaf.
a brown squirmy inchworm	I thought of the time when my brother, my cousins Eddie, Elliot, Lisa and I went into the night crawler business. My brother Andy and Eddie would stand in front of a sign made by Lisa and yell "Night crawlers! Thirty-six cents a dozen. . . ."

Portraits in verse are also a splendid spur to creativity. I explain that I do not want poems telling me that the child's friend or mother or uncle is "nice" or "good" or "pretty" or "handsome" or "funny," but poems that show what kind of a person it is through that person's activities. Again, I repeat my admonition that a reader has intelligence, and the writer must show enough about the person so that the reader can draw his own conclusions about what sort of person it is. Edna St. Vincent Millay's "Portrait of a Neighbor" starts us off. For the older children, Robert Frost's "The Death of the Hired Man" leads to portraits done through conversation.

I do not believe in the filling-in of blanks, as a general rule, or the gimmicky aids that give a child a beginning to be completed. But occasionally an idea spontaneously suggested in class will spark creativity. I remember that when one student pressed me for something to write about I gave her a line that had been bumping around in my head for about twenty years. I explained that I had never been able to work it into a poem; perhaps she could. She could and she did as she went for a walk one day.

The media offer to some children a chance to express their feelings—from praise for certain books or television programs or movies to downright criticism and disdain of commercials. Children are well aware of the idiocy of many commercials and like to invent their own of a nonsensical nature. News events, as well, provide outlets—for thoughts about war or outer space or (*rara avis*) a happy occasion such as a sporting event. After such events we have spent weeks studying and writing ballads. The reading aloud of Elizabeth Bishop's "The Ballad of the Burglar of Babylon" is a pertinent beginning for this kind of expression.

Very often we play records, but not the sort on which a

potpourri of "selected" (and I daresay outmoded) poetry is thrown together. There is a pop song that begins, "As I was walking down the street one day." It sparked, in a group of older children whose attention was poor and whose imaginations had been neglected, a rash of similar "songs," some of which were sung, to guitar accompaniment, in class. I have always encouraged children to bring whatever poems, songs, or books they have enjoyed to share with the others, and it is heartening to see how literary taste can be improved through this sort of sharing. If I am astounded at the paucity of good poetry in most homes, at least I can walk to the poetry shelves in the library and send each child home with a good poetry anthology or work of a single poet through which to browse.

A copy of Carl Sandburg's *Wind Song* or Walt Whitman's *Leaves of Grass* can work absolute wonders for the child who will not abandon meaningless rhyme. *A Little Laughter*, compiled by Katherine Love, or the many humorous anthologies of William Cole can cause the child who thinks of poetry only as Beauty, Truth, and Wisdom to think of the power of levity in new terms. Horace Gregory's *The Crystal Cabinet* can help the child who is poor at hearing meter begin to hear the cadence and music of poetry. *Sprints and Distances*, compiled by Lillian Morrison, is a perfect answer for the sports-oriented boy, as is Helen Plotz's *Imagination's Other Place* for the science- or fact-oriented student. And for the child who thinks poetry is some sort of strange language, there are Sara Hannum and Gwendolyn Reed's *Lean Out the Window* and *Don't You Turn Back*, the poetry of Langston Hughes chosen by Lee Bennett Hopkins. These are only a few of the fine anthologies available today. *I Am the Darker Brother*, compiled by Arnold Adoff, Blanche Thompson's *All the Silver*

Pennies, David Mackay's *A Flock of Words*, Robert Hayden's *Kaleidoscope*, Nancy Larrick's *Piping Down the Valleys Wild*, Herbert Read's *This Way Delight*, Frances Monson McCullough's *Earth Air Fire and Water*—all these and more I have introduced to children.

On days when none of us feel much like serious work, we can write nonsense verse:

SASSAFRAS

Glu-arp.
Oggle de biggle, snizzle de priz.
Whatchamacallet, hoodledebop.
Frizzily bloorping, frassity toop.
Crack ip ily fropping.
Schnorkeley schnopping.

Margot

Children usually enjoy the writing of epigrams and epitaphs. Lloyd contributed an epitaph for a collection of writing we mimeographed for our Extended Day Class:

"Here I lie
under a great
tombstone—
with etchings on it
that I can't understand for the world . . .
by the Creative Writing class,
a jumble of words—
but the book looks pretty anyway!"

Epitaphs may sound a bit grisly for third-graders, but by seventh grade, at least, the children enjoy reading and writing them. Lloyd's effort was intended to poke fun at his own "etchings" which were included in the book.

Another great favorite of mine is the cautionary rhyme,

for it is not only amusing to most children, but it strikes a note that hits close to home. A reading of "Jim" by Hilaire Belloc, as well as other selections from his work, or Maurice Sendak's *Pierre,* or the Struwwelpeter rhymes, can send children off on a whole series of cautionary rhymes spelling out a comeuppance for their own faults—going to bed too late, not wearing a jacket, procrastinating, staying too long on the telephone. It further serves as a basis for the discussion of the horrors of didactic, "preaching," and "message" poems.

Parody, for the more sophisticated child, can be riotous fun. I have enjoyed it so much myself that it actually became the reason for compiling *Speak Roughly to Your Little Boy.*

I find that an occasional game breaks the monotony. We have often played a game described by Laurence Housman in *My Brother, A. E. Housman:* an "evening diversion" would be the writing of a poem based on nouns, one supplied by each person present. The nouns given were "hat," "novel," "banker," "cucumber," "yacht," and "abridgement." "Obviously," writes Laurence Housman, "the last was the crux; and this is how Alfred tackled it":

> At the door of my own little hovel
> Reading a novel I sat;
> And as I was reading the novel
> A gnat flew away with my hat.
> As fast as a fraudulent banker
> Away with my hat it fled,
> And calmly came to an anchor
> In the midst of the cucumber-bed.
>
> I went and purchased a yacht,
> And traversed the garden-tank,

And I gave it that insect hot
When I got to the other bank,
Of its life I made an abridgement
By squeezing it somewhat flat,
And I cannot think what that midge meant
By flying away with my hat.

Some of the other ideas that have worked well from time to time include assignments to observe animals. Most children, if they do not have a pet of their own, make trips to the zoo occasionally or know of someone who has a pet. As noted previously, cats can be a great favorite, but dogs, turtles, horses, and fish offer unlimited possibilities. The cat poems and tide pool poems, as well as poems on the aquarium at University Elementary School, attest to the popularity of animal poems. At the same time, one can read poems about animals, including the Neruda and Whitman selections.

Another idea, and a good tool to free children from factual statement, is the writing of Love or Hate poems. Children, we seem finally to have recognized, do have loves and hates, and they vary with each child. We have used many of these poems throughout this book. These are not poems that begin "I hate" or "I love," but rather those that express feelings for the richness of life, or the hypocrisies and ecological concerns of today's child.

Oftentimes I bring *ABC* picture books to a classroom. They are surprisingly popular with the older children. Writing creatively about the alphabet can range from sheer nonsense to expressions of feelings about certain words and sounds.

Many times something observed by one child and shared with the class will inspire others to make similar observations. A boy who turned in an observation about the curtains in his room was met, the next week, by an entire class writing about *their* curtains and drapes. These ranged from "long and tailored curtains" through "torn curtains" to "drapes pulled uneven" and theater curtains that "hide the play."

Children who are studying foreign languages can often find pleasure in translating the simplest of poems and thereby becoming more familiar with the power of words well expressed.

In order to free thoughts, to make them less factual and more fluid, I have often played a record of James Joyce reading from *Finnegans Wake*. The assignment I then make suggests to the children that we let our thoughts flow freely, without worying about writing full sentences. Some amusing contributions have come from this:

> I am thinking about the fact that pencils can write on a vertical surface, but pens can't because the ink flows backwards. Now that I see a box (a cigar box) shut says Corina Viva with a little encircled R at the lower right hand corner and I think how commercial life is. I see my lizard cage and my lizard buried deep in the new gravel I got him last week and just looking at the advantages and disadvantages of being a lizard. This makes me think about Benson & Hedges 100's which takes me back to commercials and stuff . . . I am doing this at night in bed inside with a little distraction downstairs called music and getting mad at myself for waiting until the last night when I had all of Christmas vacation to do it, and that I'm going to have to do the whole assignment over because I blew it. . . .
>
> *Steve*

229

Almost library . . ug-uggy . . . sometimes fink glasses
when get contacts everyone talking how I think going
Joy's stain on shirt shut up Jon Dods! Running out
good library books Someone passed out pink sheet
looks dull Can't think! Head aches gotto stop now
Mrs. M. talking should be listening. . . . .

Anna

In recent years I have been experimenting with concrete
poetry by children. Though I have never been able to decide exactly what concrete poetry is, I have some clues
through the remarks of concretists. Mary Ellen Stolt says
that its "concentration upon the physical material from
which it is made" determines its name. Eugene Wildman
tells us that it "aims, in general, at the ideogrammatic state."
I tend to think of it in terms of a "shape poem" for children, wherein the appearance of what they see determines
how the poem will form itself. I cannot say that anything
the children have done is poetry, but I do find the idea invaluable in weaning children away from meaningless rhyme.

<pre>
        The question mark is
        very bothersome. It
        raises so many questions.
     It has   to
     know   everything,
                               Just like
                               a nagging
                               neighbor,
                              it pops
                              up when
                              you don't
                              particularly
                              care for it.
</pre>

The scoundrel's
shape further
angers you,
for what does
it look like?
There's that
question mark

again! He
just keeps
coming up!
            Jared

Lisa, at the Beverly Hills Library Creative Writing Club, went out for a walk and came back with

At the third-grade level, children enjoy shape poems. Boys especially like poems they can do in the shape of a baseball, a football, or a baseball diamond or football playing field. A ball spinning in air suggests that they write the words around in a maze. Indeed, sometimes if the paper is large enough, the plays of an entire game are described! Girls are more apt to portray rain falling in drops or the shape of a garden.

Occasionally, a child will be able to approach the making of a poem in this form, but its chief value is certainly that it frees one from having to use rhyme and forces one to think of poetry in terms other than nature and beauty. Anything can be the subject of a poem!

It would be difficult for me to think of a time when the teacher might run out of ideas to suggest to children. A constant reading of poetry from anthologies will always spark the child with ideas, provided the reading is broad and the child's emotions are kept in mind. As we learn to know the children we teach, we become aware of the individual interests of each, and we must capitalize on these interests.

I have always refused to believe that there is a child who can find nothing to write about. A child's imagination may be undernourished by the circumstances in which he finds himself, but it becomes necessary, then, to feed and nurture it. And if our own imaginations become impoverished, then it is time for us, as teachers, to feed them—for we have only to take a walk ourselves, sometimes looking no farther than our feet and the ground upon which we walk. If we end up at the library and browse through the hundreds of volumes that speak to young people in many ways, so much the better.

This must be our commitment.

17: The Stamp, the Teacher, the Open Door

The little silver box opened and there it was, pressed against the purple ink pad, like a bird in its nest. What a delight when, after holding it for a moment against the fine white and mauve palm of my hand, the stamped words appeared:

FRANCISCO RUIZ

MOGUER.

How I envied that stamp of my school friend in Don Carlos' School! With a small home printing set that I found in the attic in an old desk, I tried to make one with my name. But it did not come out right, and, in particular, it was difficult to get an impression. It was not like the other one which such ease left here and there, in a book, on the wall, on one's flesh, its legend:

FRANCISCO RUIZ

MOGUER.

One day there came to my house, with Arias the silversmith from Seville, a traveling salesman of desk accessories. What a ravishing array of rulers, compasses, colored inks, and stamps! They were of all shapes and sizes. I broke my savings bank and with a duro I found I ordered a stamp with my name and town. What a long week that was. What heart flutterings when the mail arrived. What a disappointment when the postman's footsteps passed our house in the rain. At last, one night, he brought it. It was a small complicated gadget, with pencil, pen, initials for sealing wax . . . what not! And when I touched a spring, the stamp appeared, brand new, shining bright.

Was anything left unmarked in my house? What was not mine? If someone borrowed the stamp, "Careful! It will wear out!" What anguish! The following day with what gladsome haste I carried everything to school, everything—books, smock, hat, shoes, hands, marked with the legend:

JUAN RAMÓN JIMÉNEZ

MOGUER.

TO READ THESE PARAGRAPHS from *Platero and I* to children with whom you are sharing creative writing is to say to each one, use your own eyes, your own ears, your own sense of smell and touch. Write down what you feel; for as Juan Ramón Jiménez stamped everything with his name, so must you use your name, your individuality. You must say what you have to say to the world by letting it know how you feel and react. You must dig long and hard into your own imagination, use all of your faculties, sensitivities, and reactions, create your own fresh and new images for all of us to share.

You will be learning something of how a poet writes, how he makes the words of his poem tell you something of his feelings. You will be learning about the forms, the elements that go into the making of a poem, so that you may use these elements too. While you are learning you will be writing your own words and thoughts and feelings. If what you have written is really a poem, it will speak with a force, a voice, that others will recognize as something unique and yet universal. And they will know that you have spoken truly.

Through the writing of poetry, you will also be helping yourself to grow, for although you may not produce a great poem, one that is worthy of publication, you will be learning something of the shape, both literally and figuratively, of your experience, your own emotions, and how you feel about things. You will be talking to yourself, in a sense, and through reshaping your thoughts and sensuous experiences, you will arrive at a better and more meaningful response to all about you.

You will learn, too, that your imagination can be harnessed and put to good use. You will learn that you have sensitivities that have been given to no other child or man. You will learn that being able to create is one of the greatest joys of life, dependent upon no other person but yourself.

You will find that what you have written one day is not good enough for the next; you must not copy yourself or others. You will find that you must trust your own thoughts. You will also find that the rules you follow, the elements you choose in making your own poems, differ from the rules and elements of others. You will find that there is no secret formula for this creation; it is for each of you to discover for yourself.

You may also discover that regardless of your standing in a class, whether you have been endowed with unusual brain power, or more ordinary, you can write a poem. You have the imagination and feeling to do so. You grow, not through the learning of fact alone, of classification, or of the right answers for a test, but through your own special experiences in life.

You will also learn that while you are learning to trust and explore your own emotions and experiences, you must also learn something of the rules that govern your expression. If you do not learn to give shape to these thoughts, through forms that make your thoughts worth sharing, you have cheated others by your lack of communication; but mostly, you have cheated yourself.

We do not use these words with the children we teach. But we are mindful of them with each new face that comes into our classroom. We are looking and listening for the right moment to bring out each of these points. We are reading literature to emphasize what we wish to say. We are patiently waiting for the voice of the child to be heard and at the same time offering the tools, the forms which will enhance that voice, give it force and credence.

We are apt to be lonely, for we do not live in a time or place, alas, that encourages this individuality. We are living in a time when many men find it easier and more expedient to level us, child and teacher alike, to a norm— when men would prefer that we read the same books, hear the same news, think the same thoughts. Our great American dream, that every person should have an education, has played us some cruel tricks along the way.

Many educators, most unfortunately, are more interested in standards, in test scores, in grades. The children must get in to college at all costs. There is no time for creativity. It is discouraged. It is even ignored. What masquerades as creativity is nothing more than rhyming verses to prove that we can all hear sounds the same way. It is mimicking lofty thoughts and platitudes that adults want to hear. It is factual statements, to prove that we have comprehended the textbooks. It is counting syllables. It is long strings of adjectives or an outpouring of pointless metaphors and similes.

May Swenson, a distinguished poet, tells us:

> At one time, wishing to clarify to myself the distinction between poetry and other modes of expression, I put down these notes:
>
> Poetry doesn't tell; it shows. Prose tells.
>
> Poetry is not philosophy; poetry makes things be, right now.
>
> Not an idea, but a happening.
>
> It is not music, but it sounds while showing.
>
> It is mobile; it is a thing taking place—active, interactive, in a place.
>
> It is not thought; it has to do with senses and muscles.
>
> It is not dancing, but it moves while it remains.
>
> . . . And it is not science. But the experience of poetry is animated with the insatiable curiosity of science. The universe, inside and out, is properly its laboratory. More plain than ever before is the potent fact that we are human particles in a culture of living change. We must either master the Great Whirl or become victims of it. Science is unavoidably reshaping our environment and in the future will prominently influence the next development of individual man and his species. Art, more intimately, deals with and forms the emotional and spiritual climate of our experience. Poetry can help man to stay human.

We, the teachers, must also believe that creative writing, in an age so technically oriented, can help our children to stay human. And toward that end we commit ourselves to a sort of teaching for which no textbook or teacher's guide can ever be written. There are no correct answers; no chapter outlines; no summary questions to fall back upon. We must each make our way, faltering at times, but strengthened by the knowledge that we have allies in the past and in the contemporary voices we are hearing and in the resurgence of creativity today.

We need to try to answer the question put by Dr. Harold Taylor:

> Where is there room for the students whose gifts are not purely scholastic? Where is there room for the child who loves to paint, to sculpt, to sing, to act, to compose, to write, to dance, to celebrate his personal joy? Or, for that matter, where is there in the educational system a concern for the majority of American children whose interest and aptitudes in the arts are not yet formed and who need for their personal development that kind of direct experience with the arts which alone can nourish their sensibilities and cultivate in them a devotion to cultural values?

Myra Cohn Livingston

BORN IN OMAHA, *Nebraska, Myra Cohn Livingston shared her happy childhood with dozens of
neighborhood children and spent her summers with
cousins who lived out of town. She began writing
poetry at an early age, wrote plays produced in
school, and also showed talent for music. In 1937
the family moved to Los Angeles, where Mrs. Livingston continued her writing by working on the
high school newspaper and her music by perfecting
her French-horn playing and winning a Music Educators' National Competition. Then she entered
Sarah Lawrence College, where she studied writing
under Katherine Liddell, Hortense Flexner, Robert
Fitzgerald, and Horace Gregory.*

*After her marriage, Mrs. Livingston continued to
write—in particular, poetry for children—and has
published several collections of her own verse as well
as anthologies of which she is the editor. She is
deeply interested in education, particularly the fostering of creativity in young people. Among her
many teaching experiences have been classes at the
Beverly Hills Public Library; a class in rock poetry
and writing at the Beverly Hills Continuation
School; and an experimental class in creative writing
at UCLA's University Elementary School. She is
Poet in Residence for the Beverly Hills Unified
School District.*

*Mrs. Livingston, her husband Richard R. Living-
ston, and their three children, Josh, Jonas, and Jennie live in Beverly Hills, California, where—besides
lecturing, reviewing books, and being active in the
PTA and the Friends of the Beverly Hills Public
Library—she is much caught up in the rearing of
dogs, the theater, antique and classic cars, sports car
rallies, goldfish, the raising of camellias, and beach
bumming at Malibu.*